IRENE ECONOMIDES

Bachelor of Political Sciences and Theology
Guide - Lecturer of the Hellenic Tourism

THE TWO FACES OF GREECE

(A civilisation of 7.000 years)

ATHENS
1989

Cover:

- Painting by Raffaele Ceccoli, National Art Gallery of Athens. The Acropolis in the beginning of the XIX c.
- National Festival of "25 March" 1985 in the village Eratini, in the area of Delphi. Photo: Irene Economides

Dedicated
to the new Philhellenes

Greece

"Yet are thy skies as blue, thy crags as wild;
Sweet are thy groves, and verdant are thy fields;
Thine olive ripe as when Minerva smiled,
And still his honied wealth Hymettus yields;
There the bleth bee his fragrant fortress builds,
The free-born wanderer of thy mountain air;
Apollo still thy long, long summer guilds,
Still in his beam Pendeli's marbles glare:
Art, Glory, Freedom fail, but Nature still is fair"

Lord Byron *"Child Harold's Pilgrimage*
(C.II, LXXXVII)

Haidee, a Greek girl. Engraving after the painting by Ch. L. Eastlake, Athens, Benaki Museum, 27646. She inspired Lord Byron, who is describing her in "Don Juan", C. III, LXX, LXXII, LXXIII.

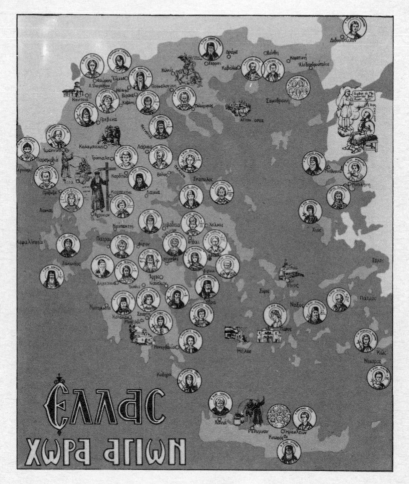

Greece: country of Saints. Greece gave millions of saints. Some of the most important are shown on this map. This picture was taken from the book "The wounded Virgin" - Monastery of Vatopedi, Mt. Athos.

Introduction

The people who has always lived on the lace-like peninsula, at the South-East of Europe which the Romans called Greece, but whose real name is Hellas (the prefix - hel means "holy" or "sunny"), this people has always had a deep attachment to their country, and a deep need to keep this country free, developing at the same time a spirit of universality.

In spite of different conquests of the land, due partly to its strategic importance and partly to certain shortcomings of the people themselves, the Greeks or the Hellenes never lost the sense of their national continuity through the different periods of their long and awe-inspriring history. And the various aspects of their long civilisation possess some common characteristics which compose the innermost depth of the Greek soul, identifiable in the pagan, as well as in the Christian period, in times of freedom or slavery, of glory or suffering.

These common characteristics that we encounter during a civilisation of 7.000 years are the following:

a) A sense of harmony and symmetry. Both of these words are of Greek origin, because the Greeks first conceived these values and they have passed intact into all European languages.

b) A sense of measure ("metro" in Greek from which the English word "metric" derives). The Greeks had a horror of excess ("hubris"), because they knew that excess was always punished by the Divine.

c) A love for colour and for precise form, seen not only on master pieces such as the reliefs of the classical Parthenon, but also on simple articles of every day use such as a Neolithic vase of Thessaly.

d) A sense of beauty, which after the magnificent balance it achieved in the classical era of the V c. B.C., in the Byzantine period it

9

soared to the "sublime" and found its transcedental expression in the spiritual beauty of the Christian Orthodox faith and became spiritual beauty, which leads, in the Byzantine art, to the presence of the Holy Trinity: the source of life and of every Goodness. The Holy Trinity, the One Living God of the Bible, transmits to the sincere believers, the "non created energies" (through the right participation at the Holy Sacrements) for sanctification of the world and the final glorification of Man and of all the Universe (Rev. 21).

It seems today miraculous how all these virtues of the Greek civilisation have been inherited from generation to generation without any break; and it seems even more miraculous when we study it in the light of the sufferings of the long Turkish occupation, when regular schooling was missing totally because of prohibition of the barbarian conqueror. The people who had given the lights to the rest of the world remained for centuries without education, except for some "secret schools" in the monasteries and four schools of university level (one of them at Constantinople, founded immediately after the fall of the Byzantine empire). These schools kept the flame of Hellenism alive till the marvelous moment of the Independence (1830).

The proof that the same people continues to live in this country, where his ancestors had lived in antiquity and in the Middle Ages (Byzantine period) is the following:

a) **the language:** Philologists have demonstrated that 60% of the vocabulary, living on the lips of modern Greeks, is Homeric (the language of the Iliad and the Odyssey).

b) Recent anthropological studies have proved **the racial continuity** of the population of Greece through all the periods till now. (Angel J.L. & Poulianos Aris). (Poulianos Aris: "The origin of the Greeks", Athens 1968).

c) **The biological characteristics** are far more important than the two methods mentioned above, because by studying the genetic distance we can see the historical evolution, not only of one nation, but of the whole humanity. Among these characteristics the most important is the genetic system HLA: (Human Leucocyte Antigen).

The HLA antigens are inherited in a stable way, they appear

since the beginning of life, and continue to be stable during life.

The study of the Greek Doctor Z. Polimenidis (Doctorate, Salonica, 1978) presents the genetic distance between the Greeks and other nations as given by the following Table:

GENETIC DISTANCE

Greeks — Swiss	893
Greeks — French	919
Greeks — Italians	1089
Greeks — Russians	1298
Greeks — Danish	1422
Greeks — Spanish	2011
Greeks — Germans	2293
Greeks — English	2316
Greeks — Hebrews	3033
Greeks — Arabs	4146
Greeks — Turks	5007

According to this genetic distance the Greek population ressembles the Caucasian (European) type, while at the same time it presents **certain individual characteristics.** (Each nation has its own HLA characteristics).

In addition the great difference in the genetic distance between the Greeks and the Turks, according to the Table above, proves that the 400-year Turkish domination did not influence the Greek race at the biological point of view.

d) **The folk tradition:** Folk danses and poetry, music, decorative patterns in art (stone, wood, embroideries), traditional architecture, all underline the historical continuity of Hellenism.

e) **Certain virtues and shortcomings of the Greeks** persistent from the time of the Iliad and the Odyssey till our days. The virtues profoundly rooted are: the love for their father-land, the deep religious feeling, strong family ties, the love for progress, the artistic and creative spirit, the flexible and vivid thinking and the

11

spirit of hospitality and inventiveness.

As for the shortocomings, those are: the eternal political disputes, which have often led to desasters after great glories and a self pride too touchy, that very seldom accepts the superiority of another person. For example the wrath of Achilles in the Iliad which nearly made the Greeks lose the war.

During the Turkish domination some more shortcomings were added, because of the long obscurity of four centuries without regular education, and after the Independence the sudden invasion of the Western ways and customs, that the Greek people was not yet ready to receive and assimilate, nominally the Occidental governors (foreign Kings and occidental administration system), are suffocating the long local tradition.

Neverthless we cannot but be optimistic about the future of this people, when we think of the marvelous power of assimilation that he possess and which gave through the millenia so many examples of absorbing and transforming into something new of what influences he received. (The different aspects of his long civilisation was a synthesis of various influences that this people received through the centuries at this critical crossroads where he is living). Plato already in the IV c. B.C. had said "The Greeks hellenize whatever they receive from the barbarians" (foreigners). And a modern Greek writer has remarked: "From the ancient Hellenic soul important traces have remained in the inner self of the Greeks, and this Hellenic soul which is humane, free and generous, is not dead". (Those who are alive", J. Dragoumis, 1878-1920).

Let us hope that some day the historical conditions will be favorable and will enable the Hellenic nation (rich in possibilities), to create a new synthesis which may well lead to a new European Renaissance.

Someone who studied objectively the Greek civilisation and history said: "You the Greeks you will remain the youth of the world".

Notes: The native character of the Greek people has been proved by the recent excavations of Prof. G. Korrès in Messinia, south Peloponnese, and of Prof. Theod. Spyropoulos in Arcadia central Peloponnese.
— The Genetic Distance HLA has been discovered by the French Dr. Jean Dausset, Nobel (1980).

The two faces of Greece

The civilisation of Greece is at least 7.000 years old and is divided in two parts: the pagan civilisation which lasted 5.000 years and the Christian - Orthodox civilisation, which continues till now and has an age of almost 2.000 years. So Greece has two faces: a pagan and a Christian one. This is why the civilisation of Greece has often been called Greco-Christian.

A. The Pagan Face

The Early-Stone Age

Human and animal life existed in Greece in the prehistoric Early-Stone Age, as anthropological research has proved at several places of the country.

Stone instruments have been found in the cave of Saïdi near the lake of Copaïs (Beotia), as well as in Pireus, in Thessaly, in Salonica and elsewhere. Bones of animals which do not exist any more in Greece have been found at Pikermi (Attica), in the cave of Kilada at Ermionide (South Argolis), in the island of Samos, and in the famous cave of Petralona in Chalcidice (South Macedonia), where there has been found the oldest human skull on Greek soil, and belongs to a transitional type of man that comes between the homus erectus and homus sapiens. This skull of the oldest man found till now in Greece is exhibited at the Palaeontological School of Salonica University. Most of the Palaeontological finds of Greece are exhibited in the Palaeontological Museum of Athens University (University Campus - Kaissariani). But there are some more at the Goulandri Museum of Natural History in Kifissia (Northern suburb of Athens), at the local

Trunk of a petrified tree on the island of Lesbos. (Photo of the Guide-book of Lesbos, M. Toubis, 1983.

Museum of Petralona cave, at the Palaeontological Museum of Samos, and at the Museum of Larissa (Thessaly).

A palaeontological phenomenon unique in Greece is the petrified forest at Sigri, a village on the island of Lesbos. It is 500.000 to 800.000 years old and was formed by a volcanic erruption, which has burnt an immense forest, leaving enormous petrified trunks of different colours. At the Goulandri Museum of Natural History we can see some pieces of these strange trees.

The Late-Stone Age (5.000-3.000 years B.C.)

Vestiges of the oldest civilisation on Greek soil are found in Crete, Cyprus and Thessaly (Central Greece). They date from the V millenium B.C. This civilisation has an agricultural character and the people who created it lived in settlements with a certain defensive system. This people had a primitive religion: the cult of Mother-Earth, goddess of fertility. These neolithic inhabitants of Greece were already sea-going people. This statment is proved by the discovery of tools in obsidian (black volcanic glass), in many places of the Greek mainland, as well as in Peloponnese (e.g. Museum of Olympia). But this material (the obsidian) is quarried only in the island of Melos in the Aegean Sea, so it is evident that it was transported by small boats, whose design we can see engraved on some Neo-lithic potery (Athens National Museum). Among the most beautiful works of art of this Late-stone Age civilisation are vases in ceramic of a great variety of form and decorative patterns. Other characteristic pieces of art of that period are the marble or terracota idols of Mother-Earth, the most ancient cult in the area of the Aegean Sea.

We can study these finds especially at the National Museum in Athens, where there are also exhibited objects of Cycladic art such as the two famous musicians made of white marble of the island of Paros (central Aegean Sea). So it seems that music was already known in Greece in the third millenium B.C.

Other Museums which possess interesting Late-Stone Age finds are the following: The Heraclion Museum (Crete), the Museum of Volos (South-East of Thessaly), where there is a marvelous exhibition of finds from the famous settlments of that period: Dimini and Sesclo (10 km West of Volos), and the museum of Nicosia in

15

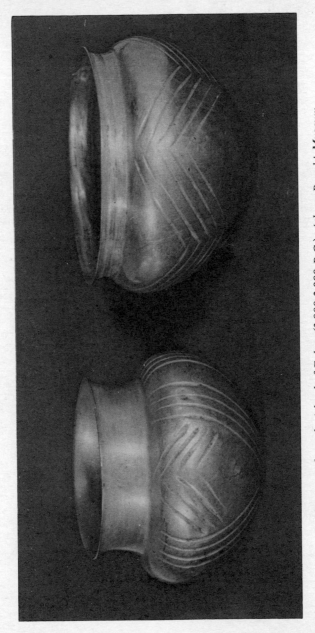

Golden cups, from the island of Eubea (3.000-2.800 B.C.), Athens Benaki Museum.

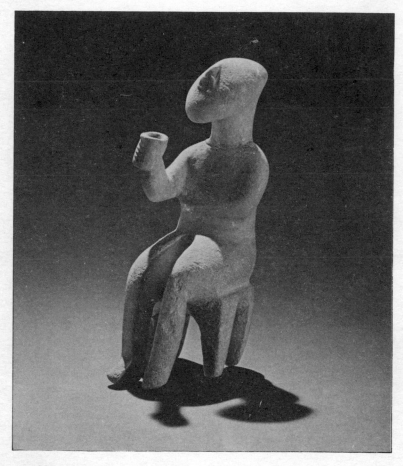

Marble Cycladic idol, late III mil. B.C. "Goulandri" Museum of Cycladic Art, Athens.

Cyprus, where we can see the finds of the celebrated Late-Stone Age settlement of Cheroketia, which goes back to an even earlier period, the VII millenium B.C.

The transitional period between the Late-Stone Age and the Bronze era is marked by a unique discovery: the palace at Lerna, which goes back to 2.000 years B.C. (near the city of Argos in Peloponnese). American excavations have brought to light its massive foundations near by the swamp, where lived Hydra, the monster which figures in one of the twelve labors of Hercules. (Interesting finds of this transitional period are also exhibited in the Museum of Tripolis in central Peloponnese).

The Bronze Era II Millenium B.C.

The archeological studies have shown that bronze started to be used at the same time in all the countries around the Mediterranean Sea towards the end of the III millenium B.C.

In Greece this period is called also Creto-Mycenean, because the two great centers of this civilisation are situated in Crete (Cnossos) and in Mycenae (Eastern Peloponnese). Those who created the Mycenean civilisation were called Aecheans, and they were one of the three most important Hellenic tribes. They possessed such a dynamism, that their civilisation spread throughout Grece (there were found Mycenean tombs 1.000 m. above sea level on Mt. Olympus, and Mycenean remmants as far as Cyprus, such as Salamis established by the brother of Ajax, and Paphos founded by the King of Arcadia Agapinor XII c. B.C. Mycenean finds have also been discovered all along the western coast of Asia Minor (Eastern Aegean) and at the coast of the Mediterranean Syria (the ancient city of Ugarit opposite Cyprus).

On the other hand the Minoans of Crete (taking their name from Minos the first legendary King of Crete) created a maritime empire in the Aegean Sea, where the influence of the Minoan civilisation can be especially seen in the island of Santorini or Thera and at Phylacope, in the island of Melos.

The Minoans had a strong fleet to protect their island, that is why towns in Crete had no fortresses. The Minoan Cretans sailed as far as Spain in their ships, in order to obtain copper, and this is how

18

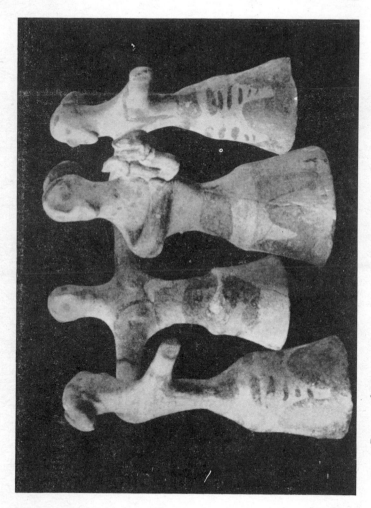

Dance of Minoan women arround a lyre-player, terracota XV c. B.C. Heraclion Museum-Crete. Similar danse can be seen in Crete today.

No.	Value	No.	Value	No.	Value	No.	Value
01	da	23	mu	45	de	67	xi
02	ro	24	ne	46	je	68	ro2
03	pa	25	a2	47		69	tu
04	te	26	ru	48	nwa	70	ko
05	to	27	re	49		71	
06	na	28	i	50	pu	72	pe
07	di	29	pu2	51	du	73	mi
08	a			52	no	74	ze
09	se	30	ni	53	ri	75	we
10	u	31	sa	54	wa	76	ra2
11	po	32	qo	55	nu	77	ka
12	so	33	ra3	56	pa3	78	qe
13	me	34		57	ja	79	zu
14	do	35		58	su	80	ma
15	mo	36	jo	59	ta	81	ku
16	pa2	37	ti	60	ra	82	
17	za	38	e	61	o	83	
18		39	pi	62	pte	84	
19		40	wi	63		85	
20	zo	41	si	64		86	
21	qi	42	wo	65	ju	87	
22		43	ai	66	ta2		
		44	ke				

Symbols of the Linear B script.

20

they left there some elements of their civilisation: the bull-festivals, the feminine dress with panels, the hair style of women, and the huge ear-rings that we see in the magnificent frescoes in the palace of Cnossos and in the houses of Thera. This period is also called legendary, because most of the celebrated legends of the Greek Mythology were created then.

Most of the artistic remains of this period are exhibited at the National Archeological Museum in Athens (on the upper floor we also see the finds from Thera), as well as at the Archeological Museum of Heraclion in Crete, and at the Museum of Nicosia in Cyprus. The visitor is impressed by the beauty and variety of these artefacts as well as the high standard of this highly sofisticated civilisation.

The script of this period - the Linear B - has come down to us scratched on clay tablets, found in Cyprus (Arcado - Cyprian script was used there as late as the classical period), in Crete, in Mycenae and in Pylos (where we admire the best preserved Mycenean palace (south-west of Peloponnese). The decipherment of this script by M. Ventris in 1952 proved that this civilisation of the Bronze era is Greek, because the language recorded on these tablets is Greek.

Note: Writing marks the historical periods. What goes before is pre-history. So the history of Greece begins at least in the XVI c. B.C. after the discovery of the Linear-B tablets (Cyprus included).

The Iron Age Ist Millenium B.C.

The Geometric period (XI-VIII c. B.C.)

The first part of this period (XI-VIII c. B.C.) is called Geometric, because pottery all over Greece (Cyprus included) was decorated with geometric designs. Architecture and sculpture of this period were in wood. This information has come to us through ancient literary sources (e.g. Pausanias, II c. B.C.).

After the troubled political events which followed the Trojan War (late XII c. B.C.) Kingship fell and the Mycenean palaces were replaced by temples, which had the same groundplan as the palaces (divided in three rooms). So the Acropolis (in Mycenae, in Athens, in Tyrins etc.) was no longer the residence of the King, but a sunctuary

21

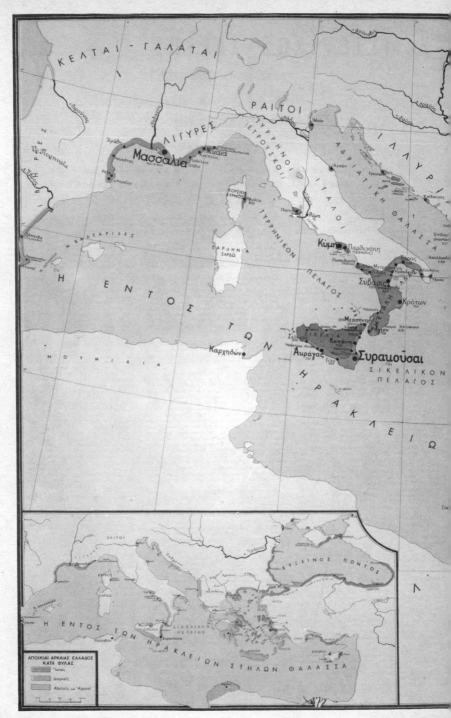

Ancient Greek colonizati

East and the West.

(foundations of early temples are to be seen on the remains of the palaces).

This is a very dark period which has been called the Middle Ages of ancient Greece (recent archeological studies have shed more light to it though). It is then that the three main Hellenic tribes: Ionians, Aecheans and Dorians, having arrived from the North of the country towards the South, mixed themselves to the local Aegean population, the Pelasgeans, forming in this way the synthesis, which has been called the "dynamic Hellenic nation". Last ·arrived the Dorians at Peloponnese, in the XI c. B.C., importing iron, which changed completely the way of living. (According to the Historian J.B. Bury 1861 - 1927 in his History of Greece, ch. I. "...the inhabitants of Arcadia, who **spoke a purely Greek language,** had been there since time immemorial").

Towards the end of this period (VIII c. B.C.) Hellenism had expanded around the shores of the Mediterranean and the Black Sea (process had already started during the II millenium B.C.) by the foundation of the famous Greek colonies.

The Greeks were the first to sail through the Dardanelles, the Bosphorus and reach the Black Sea, an event which is reflected in the legend of the Argonauts, who were the first to cross these seas on the quest of the Golden Fleece in the far-off Colchis (modern Georgia-North-East of the Black Sea). During these voyages in the Black Sea first the Greeks inaugurated fluvial navigation in the rivers (40 of them), which have their mouths around the coast of this sea.

Greece is extremely mountainous (80%). Therefore the Greeks since remote antiquity had to look for new land and travelling took them far away. Greece is also surrounded by sea, this is the reason why the foundation of their famous colonies took place along coastal areas: the eastern coast of the Aegean Sea (the famous Ionia in Asia Minor), southern Italy and Sicily ("Great Greece"), all along the Dalmatian coast, the coast of southern France and Spain, the coast of northern Africa, as well as along the coasts of the Dardanelles, the Marmora Sea, the Bosphorus and the Black Sea as far as the Crimean peninsula (modern southern Russia).

At the entrance of the Dardanelles strait, on the eastern side, is situated the peninsula called Troy in antiquity. It is there that the famous events of the Trojan War took place as they are related in

24

Greek vase (V.c. B.C.), in the Vatican Museum decorated with a scene from the legend of the "Golden Fleece", The dragon gives up Jason it had swollowed. Athena looks at her protégé in an amused way.

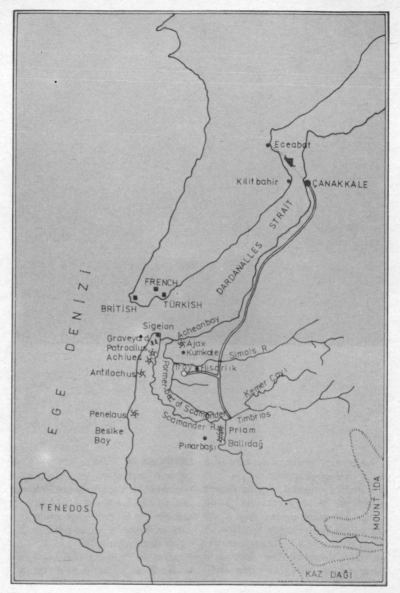

Troas peninsula (North-Eastern Aegean Sea*). The site of Ancient Troy is located near modern Hisarlik.*

The East gate, Troy VI.

the Epics of Homer the Iliad and the Odyssey (late XII c. B.C.). Homer lived about three centuries later (IX c. B.C.). He was born in Smyrna (Asia-Minor), a Greek city already in that remote period, situated opposite the island of Chios, where had also lived, and where we can see today (near the coast of the city of Chios), a stone still called "Dascalopetra" (i.e.the stone of the master) a relic of Homer's passage from Chios where he might well have sat and sing his rapsodies.

During the three centuries which followed the bewildering e-vents of the Trojan War, trobadours went from palace to palace and sang of the exploits of the heroes of the Trojan War and their virtues. Homer gave unity to this oral poetic tradition of the Hellenic nation, and he created the famous Epics of the Iliad and the Odyssey. These poems present to us all the Hellenic world with its customs, shortcomings and virtues. These Epics were first written down in the days of Pesistratus, the tyrant of Athens (dictator) in the VI c. B.C., and since then they have become the basic lesson in Greek Schools ancient and modern, and therefore the spiritual link of all the Greeks of all times.

The archeological site of Troy (Schliemann's excavations 1870-1883) can be reached either by landing at the harbour Chanakkalé on the Dardanelles (road distance 32 km). or by the coastal road of Asia Minor opposite the Greek islands of Lesbos and Chios (easy access by tourist boats during summer).

The Greek colonies soon developed into great political, scientific, philosophical and cultural centres. Their material remains we admire today especially in Ephesus, (visit by the Greek Aegean cruises, or by small boats during summer time from the islands of Samos, Chios, Lesbos and Rhodes). There are also important archeological sites in other coastal cities of Asia Minor, as Pergamum, Smyrna, Miletus, Halikarnasus etc., as well as in south Italy and Sicily, where the ancient buildings are better preserved.

During the VIII c. B.C. the Olympic Games began to be registered (ancient stone inscriptions: "Parian Marble", Oxford, Ashmolean Museum).

The first registered Olympiad dates from 776 B.C. Since then they calculated time by the Olympiads. It was their calender.

The Olympic games were celebrated every four years in the

This stone in the town of Chios, according to tradition, was seat of Homer.

Sanctuary of Zeus at Olympia (north-west Peloponnese). They were of a religious character and they aimed at the formation of perfect men physically and morally, able to defend the country in case of danger. The young men sent to Olympia from all over the Hellenic world (even from the farthest colonies), were selected among the most virtues young men of their city. The Olympic oath was also an oath of virtue.

The Geometric period ends with another poetic genious: Hesiod (750-700 B.C.). He was born in the fertile plain of Beotia, in Ascra. While pasturing the sheep of his father on the slopes of mount Helicon (residence of the Muses according to the Greek mythology), he was insprired with two great epic works: the "Theogony" and the "Works and the Days". The Muses met Hesiod there and ordered him to tell the truth. So the work of Hesiod is the first attempt at philosophical research and he has become in this way the father of Greek philosophy. (Karl Popper, the Presocratic Philosophers).

The Archaïc period (VII-VI c. B.C.)

In the VII c. B.C. they began to build temples of lime stone and make stone statues. The oldest temple of the archaïc period is in Olympia. This is the temple of Hera (Heraion) of the VII c. B.C. The temple of Apollo in Corinth and those of south Italy belong to the VI c. B.C.

The archaïc statues are very stylised and stiff, and they are characterised by a typical smile, the "archaïc smile".

The male statues are called "Kouroi" (young men), and the feminine ones are called "Korai" (young maidens). We can see them in the National Archeological Museum in Athens and in the Museum of the Acropolis. The largest Kouros is exhibited in the Museum of the island of Thasos (north Aegean Sea).

The VI c. B.C. gave also the Seven Sages of Greece (famous statesmen, or men of science), such as Solon from the island of Salamis, the great legislator and statesman of Athens. Thales of Miletus, who discovered the electric magnetism by rubing a peace of amber on wool (amber in Greek is called "electron" from which the word electicity derives), Periander the governor of Corinth under whose rule an achievement of technology was accomplished: a

Remnants of "Diolkos" on the isthmus of Corinth. We can distinguish the ruts made by the wheels of the carts.

31

The aqueduct of Eupalinos, on the island of Samos, VI c. B.C. (Photo from the «History of the Hellenic Nation" Publ. Ekdotiki", Athens 1978.

special track called Diolcos all along the Isthmus (7,5 km), in order to facilitate the passage of the ships from one harbour to the other by land. Ships were pulled along the paved road with mechanical aids. Parts of this ancient track have been discovered by excavations (1946-1958) near the modern Corinth Canal.

Another work of high technology of the Arcaïc period is the tunnel by Eupalinos of Megara. It was a subterranean aqueduct 1.000 m. long, cut through the mountain Ambelos. The tunnel was excavated simultaneously from both sides and thanks to the wise calculations of this famous architect, the two teams at work met in the middle with a vertical error of only a few feet. This tunnel which took 15 years to finish is still to be seen on the island of Samos.

During the VI c. B.C. the philosophical spirit was developped in the Ionian colonies, in the charming coasts of the eastern Aegean Sea. This philosophy is called "Presocratic", because it flourished one century before Socrates. The Ionian philosophers studied especially the material universe, its origin and function. Their studies have to do with physics, astronomy and mathematics, trying in the same time to give philosophical answers for the existance of the Cosmos, the Greek word for universe. ("cosmos" means jewel. In other words the universe is as beautiful as a jewel). This term of "Cosmos" was used for the first time by **Pythagoras,** the great Greek mathematician and philosopher (572-500 B.C.) who was born on the island of Samos, but worked mostly in south Italy, at the Greek colony of Croton.

Other important presocratic philosophers are: **Thales of Miletus (624-546 B.C.)** and his disciples **Anaximander (610-547 B.C.),** who had understood that the Earth is oscillating freely in the space (the theory of Anaximander opened the way for the studies of Aristarchus of Samos, Greek astronomer of a later period and of Copernic, as Kepler and Galileo), and **Anaximenes (550-480 B.C.),** the first to speak about monotheïsm in pagan times.

The city of Miletus where these three philosophers lived (Thales, Anaximander and Anaximenes) was one of the most famous Greek colonies, situated at the estuary of river Meander (the coast of Asia-Minor, opposite the island of Patmos). This city was so prosperous that its inhabitants founded numerous colonies (about 80 of them) on the eastern coast of the Dardanelles, the sea of Marmora

The Greek colonies located in the coastal area of Asia Minor. (Eastern Aegean Sea and Eastern Mediterranean).

*The marble avenue at the centre of Ephesus, where the philosopher
Heraclitus walked, and later on St. Paul and St. John the Evangelist.*

and the Black Sea. Miletus was a city of great maritime activity, and Thales invented certain metric systems for navigation and he had proved that the constellation of the Little Bear was indicating the North to the sailors. His study on solar eclipses was also of Great importance. He successfully predicted the eclipse of the sun in May 582.

The Presocratic philosopher however, who mostly interests modern thinkers is **Heraclitus (540-480 B.C.),** of Ephesus, another important colony, founded in the X c. B.C. by the Athenians. Heraclitus was the first to say that the universe is constantly changing except the Word: the Divine principle, which keeps the universe in harmony. (In Greek the WORD is LOGOS).

Perhaps it is not a mere coincidence that in that same city where Heraclitus had conceived the existence of the Word, there came, five centuries later, St. John the Evangelist, to write the fourth Gospel, which begins with the sentence: "In the beginning was the Word..." (John I,I).

Towards the end of the VI c. B.C. a very important event for the evolution of the Greek civilisation took place: the birth of the Athenian democracy, with the political reformation of Cleisthenes (510 B.C.). This was the transitional step towards the classical period.

The Classical period (V-IV c. B.C.)

The entrance of the classical period in history is marked by an event of fundamental importance, not only for Greece but for Europe and for all the civilised world as well. This event concerns the victories of the Greeks over the Persians in the beginning of the V c. B.C.

The Persians who at that time, constituted an immense empire, under the tyrannical despotism of King Darius, attacked small Greece, in order to punish the cities of Athens and Eretria (on the island of Eubea), because of the help they had sent to Miletus during the revolt of the Ionian colonies there against the Persian rule (499 B.C.). (These flourishing Ionian colonies had been under Lydian and Persian occupation since the middle of the VI c. B.C.).

The successful Greek resistance against the Asiatic danger

36

The common Tomb of 192 Athenian soldiers, at Marathon, who fell at this famous battle for the liberty of Greece and Europe (490 B.C.).

The pass of Thermopylae seen from the top of the hillock, where the last stand took place. On the left is Mt. Kallidromon on the right is the sea, which, in those days was closer. At the top of this hillock the traveller can read the famous epigram, composed in the V c. B.C. by Simonides, in honour of the Spartans "Stranger tell the Spartans that we lie here obedient to their laws".

saved Europe from a tyrannic totalitarianism and gave the Greeks soaring wings after the victories, enabling them to create the classical civilisation, which has constituted the basis of our Western civilisation.

The Persians, with 600 ships, started from the coast of Asia Minor, crossed the Aegean Sea and attacked Eretria first, which they destroyed. Then they crossed over to the Eastern coast of Attica and landed in the bay of Marathon (September 490 B.C.).

The Athenian army, covering the distance of 42 km in a hurry, came to meet the enemy. Ten thousand Greeks, (9.000 Athenians and 1.000 Plataeans - Beotia), defended Greece against 100.000 Persians. It was the first time in universal history that a small number of soldiers were victorious against a much larger number. At this famous battle of Marathon the Greeks fought with great valour, under Miltiades, the Athenian General who is considered the first strategic genious of Europe. The helmet he was wearing during this battle is today exhibited at the Museum of Olympia, bearing the engraved ancient inscription: "Miltiades has offered it to Zeus". He had offered it to the greatest Panhellenic sanctuary in honour of the supreme god as thanksgiving for the unexpected victory. This is an example of the deep religiosity of the ancient Greeks, and especially of their great men. Some weapons found at the battlefield of Marathon are today exhibited at the British Museum in London. The funeral lekythos offered to the Athenian soldiers killed at this battle (192 of them) are to be seen today at the Museum of Marathon.

The "Marathon race" commemorates the feat of a heroic Athenian soldier, who, immediately after the battle, ran all the way to Athens (42 km), in order to announce the victory to the Athenians who had been anxiously waiting, and the moment he had told them: "We have conquered", he fell dead.

The humiliated Persians left in their ships abandoning 6.400 dead, whom the Greeks buried respecting their religious customs. But they came back ten years later and led by their King Xerxes. After they had crossed the Dardanelles, they marched down to southern Greece, to the pass of Thermopylae, where the Greeks had come to bar their way (July 480 B.C.). The pass of Thermopylae is in central Greece on the national high-way towards Lamia, where a bronze statue of Leonidas comemorates the famous battle. (At this pass 4.000 Greeks were killed during the first Persian attacks).

After the betrayal of Ephialtes, the Greeks fought heroicaly to the last, knowing that they were surrounded by the enemy and that the barbarians would pass. An event without precedent in universal history.

The last defenders of Thermopylae were the 300 Spartans under the command of Leonidas, King of Sparta, and the 700 Thespians (Beotia) who decided not to leave with the other Greeks, dismissed by Leonidas, after he had learnt of the betrayal. The Spartans were obliged to stay, because the laws of their city forbade them to abandon the battlefield. Neverthless this sacrifice is of great importance, because this delay gave time to the Greeks of the south to organise the defense and to be victorious the same year at the famous naval battle of Salamis (August 480 B.C.).

Since then Greece never stopped to defend "Thermopylaes", in other words to be obliged to affront an enemy much more powerful, in order to safeguard her liberty, and very often to be betrayed by a new "Ephialtes" or by unfaithful allies.

The island of Salamis is situated opposite the peninsula of Piraeus (to the west), and the narrow channel which separates the two coasts, is the famous strait, where the naval battle that changed the route of universal history took place.

Today small ferry-boats daily make the cross from one coast to the other at Perama.

The sea-battle of Salamis started at dawn and finished in the evening. That day 400 Greek ships under the command of the Athenian General Themistocles defeated 1.200 Persian ships. The result of this battle was the total destruction of the Persian navy. This event is presented in a poetic way by the Athenian dramatic poet Aeschylus in his tragedy "the Persians", as he had been an eyewitness of the battle. So he heard with his own ears the enthousiastic hymn that the Greeks sang on starting the attack:

"On, ye sons of Hellas!
Free your native land,
free your children,
your wives, the fanes of your fathers' gods
and the tombs of your ancestors.
Now you battle for your all".

("The Persians" 402-405)
Ed. Harvard-Heineman

One year later, in August 479 B.C. Greece gave the last battle on its territory against the Persian army. Thirty one Greek cities, like one soul, under the command of the Spartan General Pausanias, fought at the foot of mount Kitheron at Plataea in Beotia, in order to keep their country and all Europe free.

Mardonius the Persian General and member of the Persian royal family was killed at the battlefield, a decesive fact for the Greek victory. That same year, and only a few days after this great event, the Greek fleet chased the Persians as far as the shores of Asia Minor and succeeded in destroying the Persian army camped under mount Mycale, opposite the island of Samos. So the Greeks shortly after having delivered Europe from the Asiatic danger, also delivered their compatriots of Ionia from the Persian rule.

The last event which marked the end of the Persian Wars was the conquest by the Athenians of the Sestos fortress on the European coast at the entrance of the Dardanelles. This event is the starting point of the Athenian supremacy. Athens was already becoming concious of its panhellenic role.

The V c. B.C. has often been called the Golden Age of ancient Greece, because after these victories the Greek spirit gave the maximum that the human spirit has ever offered in all branches of knowledge during the pagan times, but this century can also be called the century of Freedom and Beauty: The great joy that the Greek nation experienced after these unexpected victories, as well as the enthousiasm and self-confidence that arose from their having defeated the immense Empire of the "Medes dressed in gold", made their spirit flourish. The spirit cannot blossome in slavery, only in freedom. This is why the freedom of the country has always been the supreme ideal for the Greeks. Homer says in the Iliad (XII, 243)

41

"Only one omen is best: defend our fatherland"; and a great hero of the preparative period to the Greek independence, Rigas Ferraios (1757-1798) said: "He thinks best, who thinks in freedom". Finally among the defenders of Greece in 1940, there was a man, who later became a simple guardian of the Delphic antiquities (his only schooling had been the primary school), and yet he would say: "We fought for the freedom of our family and of our fatherland". (Recently, in a questionaire of the European Common Market, to the question: "Are you ready to die for your country?" only the Greeks answered affirmatively by a big majority).

After the sufferings of the Persian Wars, (Athens was completely destroyed and the Acropolis burnt), the Greek art became more austere. The "archaïc smile" disappeared and gave its place to the "severe style" in sculpture (for example the bronze Poseidon of the National Museum in Athens and the famous Charioteer at Delphi).

Athens was gaining little by little the full development of its democracy, so beautifully analysed by Pericles in his famous funeral speach "Epitaphios", that we can read in the history of Thucydides (460-400 B.C.), the first scientific historian of the world. It was under Pericles leadership (443-429 B.C.) that the Athenian civilisation attained its climax. This is why this brilliant period has been called "Periclean Age". His personality has sealed the great monuments that were erected on the ruins left by the Persian rage, upon which shone the splendour of the Parhenon (447-438), as well as all the Athenian culture of his time. The greates geniouses in Arts and Letters were his personal friends; the architect of the Parthenon Ictinus, the sculptor of its friezes Phidias, the dramatic poet Sophocles, and the great philosopher Socrates often met at the house of Pericles and Aspacia (a woman of high culture from Miletus of Asia Minor who inspired that brilliant man).

This "Golden Age" lasted about 50 years. It was a marvelous equilibrium between thinking and feeling. It was the synthesis of exhuberance and respect of law, which lasted as long as the great honest personalities of the Athenian democracy existed. After their disappearance there began the dicline of Athens, because of the "demagogues" (false political leaders), and of the philosophical "Relativism" of the Sophists (false philosophers), which undermined

42

Ionic temple of Athena (350 B.C.) at Priene, on the river Meander, in Asia Minor, near Militus. Priene was an Athenian colony.

the foundations of the society. Democracy is a very delicate political system, which requires honesty from both sides, that of the leaders and that of the citizens. If this honesty does not exist, democracy withers, and then dictatorship comes to bring order, as the famous Greek philosopher Aristotle says in his "Republic".

This classical spledour is very well expressed by the Parthenon, which now stands as the symbol of the European civilisation, a civilisation that is based on freedom: the freedom of the country, the freedom of law-abiding citizens and the freedom of thought. We can also admire today the classical achievement in the artistic works of the main archeological museums of Greece (Athens, Delphi, Olympia). In literature we can enjoy the flowering of the classical spirit in many editions (in English translation, even paper-backs) of philosophical, poetical, historical, rhetorical and scientific works. (University editions mainly).

However the jealousy of Sparta of the glory of Athens was such that finaly a war started between Athens and Sparta and their allies, the famous Peloponesian war (related by the historian Thucydides), which lasted about 30 years (431-404 B.C.). The result of this long war was the defeat of Athens by Sparta. Sparta soon gained the hatred of the ancient Greek world, because of its tyrannic rule, and it was defeated in its turn by the two great Generals of Thebes Epaminondas and Pelopidas. After the two Theban victories over the Spartans, one at Leuctra (Beotia), 371 B.C. and the other in Mantinea (Arcadia - Central Peloponnese) in 362 B.C., when Epaminondas lost his life, supremacy past to the city of Thebes till 338 B.C., when the Thebans and all the Greeks of the south were finaly defeated by the King of Macedonia (northern Greece) Philip II, the father of Alexander the Great, at the famous battle of Chaeronea.

The victory of Philip at Chaeronea (338 B.C.) was an event of great importance, because he united under his sceptre the previously divided Greeks. This political unity of the Greeks helped them to begin a new chapter in their history under the command of Alexander the Great, who became King at the age of twenty. He led the Greeks to the depths of Asia by an incredible and unique in world history campaign.

In spite of the fact that the IV c. B.C. was a troubled period, the

Arts and Letters were of extreme fineness and elegance. So the classical period ended with a great refinment of thought and a great hope for the future under the sceptre of Alexander the Great (336-323 B.C.).

Very elegant buildings were erected such as the Tholos of Delphi, the temples at Epidaurus and the fine temples of Asia Minor (Ionia), whereas great sculptors such as Praxiteles, Scopas and Lysyppus produced masterpieces, among which the most famous is Hermes of Praxiteles (Museum of Olympia), and a magnificent relief of a column-base of the Artemission in Ephesus (British Museum in London). This relief is expressing all the religious mysticism of that time. (The Artemission of Ephesus was one of the "seven wonders" of the world, from which only one column exists in site.

The philosophical thought of this period is especially marked by the Athenian philosopher Plato (428-347 B.C.) and Plato's disciple Aristotle (384-322 B.C.) who came from Stageira in Chalcidice (Macedonia). Both promoted pure philosophy (philosophy means love of wisdom), which is a sincere search after truth. The philosophical thought of the Greeks was so advanced during the V and IV c. B.C. that this honest effort for the discovery of truth almost reached the truth of the Gospel.

During the Roman persecutions against the Christians the philosopher and martyr St. Justin (100-165 A.D.) in his second apology said that the Greek philosophers and especially Plato had expressed "seeds of the Word" (the "spermatic Word"). In other words they had expressed some parts of the Christian truth.

On reading today some texts of the classical Greek writers one is really astonished by the clarity of their thinking, in spite of the fact that they were living in a pagan world. The same astonishement felt the Fathers of the Church, who had studied Greek philosophy, and had discovered a positive approach of it to the Christian truth. Saint Basil the Great, bishop of Caesaria in Cappadocia (IV c. A.D.) advised the Christian youth of his time to read the classical Greek writers by chosing what is best in those texts, selecting as bees do the "best honey". And St. Clement of Alexandria (II-III c. A.D.) said that the Greek philosophy had educated the pagans of the Hellenic tradition, as the Law had educated the ancient Hebrews, in order to prepare them to receive Christ. An extract from a lost tragedy of

Sophocles (V c. B.C.) mentioned by the Father of the Church Theodoret of Cyrus (Syria V c. A.D.) recalls the first verses of the Genesis:

"One, truly, one is God
who created heaven and the large earth,
the joyful sea and the power of the winds"
(Migne P.G. 83, 1005)

Even Socrates prophesied in his Apology before the Athenian judges, who had condemned him for sacrilege and sentenced him to drink the hamelock:

"God will have pity on you, and He will send
someone from above to save you."
(Plato, Apology 31a)

These words were heard during the trial at the Law-court of Heliaea (6.000 elected judges), and whose water clock was discovered during the excavations at the Athenian Agora. Socrates was condemned in 399 B.C. by an Athens in decay, and which later repented for this crime. One can see Socrates' prison today at the south-east corner of the Athenian Agora.

Neverthess, very soon, this blood-stained by the civil wars Greece, undermined by the Relativism of some false philosophers, entered a period of Renaissance. In 334 B.C. Alexander the Great crossed the Dardanelles with 30.000 soldiers from all over Greece (except Sparta), and 5.000 horsemen to conquer Asia, in order to stop once for all the Asiatic danger against Europe; and to transmit the Hellenic civilisation to the as yet uncivilised countries of the East, establishing in this way a lasting peace. The campaign of Alexander the Great in Asia (334-323 B.C.) had a civilising goal. This is why before leaving he offered sacrifices to the Nine Muses who symbolised the Arts and Sciences. The Iliad of Homer was his bedside book and men of science were with him, who would study the acquired countries. In his victorious advance he established many new cities; these were Greek cities in which the local population, which had been in a state of servitude before, received citizenship. So after his famous victories against the powerful Persian army (600.000 soldiers), he crossed the river Indus (north-west of India), and

Telmesos of Lycia. Greek tombs carved in the rock, late IV c. B.C. near Myra, south Asia Minor.

Alexander the Great on his horse. Relief of the famous sarcophagus of Sidon, called "Alexander's sarcophagus", late IV c. B.C. Archeological Museum of Constantinople. (Photo of the Military History of the Hellenes 1968).

The "Cape of the Swallows" in Pamphylia (eastern Mediterranean), where the sea unexpectedly ebbed away and let the army of Alexander the Great pass, an instance reminding the crossing of the Red Sea by the Jews. Publ. "History of the Hellenic Nation", (Vol. IV) Ekdotiki, Athens, 1973.

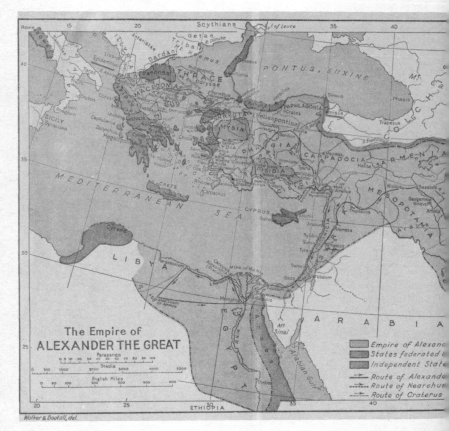

Map of Alexander the Great's campaign in Asia

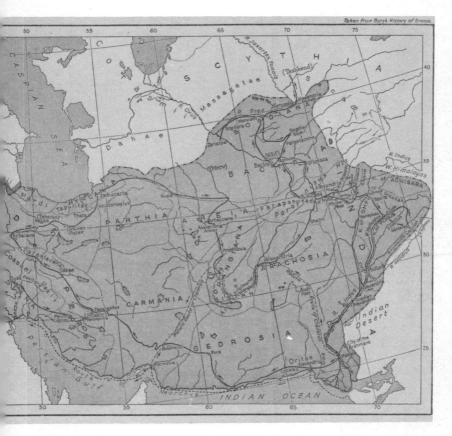

ormation of his Empire in 9 years, 334-323 B.C.

51

reached the end of the world (as they believed in those days). He stopped near the river Hyphasis (Beas), because his army refused to go further. This heroic army, that had followed him so faithfully, was now exhausted after eight years of war when their clothes were torn to shreds and the hoofs of the horses were used to the flesh. Alexander died very young after a serious illness at Babylon, in 323 B.C. But his gigantic achievement had opened the way to civilisation for humanity. The Greek language had become the universal language of that time, and this paved the way for the spreading of the Gospel.

The Hellenistic period (late IV - III & II c. B.C.)

The name Hellenistic has been given to this period because of the great expansion of Hellenism (language and civilisation) in Asia after the conquests of Alexander the Great and the formation of the Hellenistic Kingdoms by his Generals and successors: the Kingdom of Macedonia under the Antigonids, the Kingdom of Egypt under the Ptolemies, the Kingdom of Babylonia and Syria under the Seleucids, the Kingdom of Pergamum under the Attalids etc.). The capitals of these Kingdoms became great cultural and scientific centers for example Alexandria in Egypt, Pergamum at the northern coast of Asia Minor, Antioch in Syria etc. The famous library of Pergamum, rival of the one in Alexandria, possessed 200.000 volumes. Later on all volumes were offered by Antony (82-30 B.C.) to Cleopatra, the Greek queen of Egypt (68-30 B.C.) But when the Moslem Arabs entered Egypt in the VII c. A.D., they burnt the famous library of Alexandria (also containing the volumes of Pergamum), because they claimed that these books were not useful as all wisdom existed in the Coran! The loss of Alexandria's library was a great calamity for humanity: the loss of a great treasure of knowledge, and a self-back for progress.

The art of this period is of great elegance and a certain realism is characterising the sculpture. The excavations of the ancient Macedonian capital Pela, situated to the west of Salonica (45 km), as well as the excavations at Dion (70 km to the south of Salonica, close to Katerini, and Vergina about 80 km to the south-west of

The theatre of Pergamum, one of the most beautiful works of the Hellenistic period (seating capacity 10.000 spectators), situated on the hillside of the Acropolis, bellow the palace, the temples and the library, from which only the foundations exist today.

Seleucos I, founder of the Kingdom of the Seleucids which covered the largest part of Alexander's conquests: Babylonia and Syria. His capital Seleucia was on the river Tiger. Copy in bronze of a Hellenistic statue - Naples, National Museum. (Photo of the "History of the Hellenic Nation", vol. IV, Ekdotiki, Athens 1973.

Salonica), prove the Hellenic character of ancient Macedonia. Specimens of the Hellenistic Art are to be seen at Salonica's Archelogical Museum, at the island of Delos in the Cyclades (central Aegean), at Ephesus, at Pergamun at the Museum of Volos in south Thessaly (for painting), as well as at the National Archeological Museum in Athens.

The climax of that period took place in the III c. B.C. when many sciences flourished such as astronomy (one of these famous Greek astronomers was Aristarchos of Samos 310-230 B.C., who first put forward the view that the sun was the centre of the planetary system, a scientific truth that was not admitted in Europe till Copernicus' time 1473-1543), mathematics, physics, (Archimides lived in 287-212 B.C.), linguisitics and philology. The architecture, sculpture and painting of the Hellenistic period were later imitated in the houses of Pompeii in the Roman period.

Unfortunately these Hellenistic Kingdoms declined, because of the political conflicts of their Kings, who, being ambitious, desired to expand their sovereignty at the coast of a neighbouring Kingdom. So Rome, whose power was growing little by little, found the opportunity to interfere in the disputes and finally Greece was occupied by the Romans in the middle of the II c. B.C.

The Period of the Roman Domination (146 B.C. - 330 A.D.)

The two decisive events which marked the beginning of the Roman occupation are the following: The battle of Pydna in South Macedonia, when the last Macedonian King Perseus was defeated by the Romans under the command of Lucius Aimilius-Paulus in 168 B.C. (During three days were passing the chars of his triumph in Rome, loaded with the treasures of Macedonia), and the destruction of Corinth by the Roman General Momius (146. B.C.). The town was entirely rased to the ground and the population sold in slavery.

Neverthles, if Greece was conquered by the Romans from the material point of view, Rome in its turn, was conquered by Greece from the spiritual point of view, because the Romans adopted the Hellenic civilisation in all the fields and in this way the Greco-Roman world was formed, which lasted till the foundation of Constantinople by Constantine the Great (330 A.D.).

The old olive trees in Gethsemane garden under which Jesus Christ prayed the last night before His passion. Here He said to His Father: "Not as I want, but as you want" (Luke 26, 39).

The northern border of this Greco-Roman world was the British isles, the southern border was the northern coast of Africa, the western border the European coast on the Atlantic and the eastern Cappadocia (the easternmost part of Asia Minor), and the coasts of the Black Sea.

During the civil wars of the Romans several renowned battles took place on the soil of Greece, such as the battle of Pharsalus, where Caesar defeated Pompey in 48 B.C., a victory which made Caesar the master of the world. (The traveller who makes his way towards Meteora, via Trikkala, at the crossroads of Neon Monastirion, is in the area of Pharsalus). At the battle of Philippi in Macedonia (150 km to the west of Salonica) where Octavius and Antony defeated the republicans Cassius and Brutus in 42 B.C. And the famous naval battle of Actium, near the city of Preveza, on the coast of western Greece, when Octavian defeated the united fleet of Antony and Cleopatra in 31 B.C. The history of the Roman empire begins after this victory of Octavian at Actium. Octavian is the first Roman Emperor. This is the Emperor, who under the name "Octavian-Augustus" is mentioned in the Gospel of St. Luke (2,1), because Jesus Christ was born in his reign.

In this immense empire of the "Pax Romana" two powers prevailed: on the one side the roman legislation and administration, and on the other the Greek culture and language. Shortly they were joined by a new factor: the Apostolic teaching. The Apostles crossed the Greco-Roman world as far as its remotest limits, following the order of the risen Christ: "...Go ye therefore and teach all nations..." (Matt. 28.19), in order to bring the "Good News", the Evangelium or Gospel ("Evangelium" is a Greek word meaning "good news"). The "Good News" that the Apostles transmitted every where in the known world of that time, was the announcement of the **victory over death:** the Resurrection of Jesus Christ, which is a historical event that took place in time and in space, and which has had eye withnesses (I, Cor. 15, 3-7). The Apostles saw Christ alive for 40 days after His Crucifixion and Resurrection and they also saw His Ascension to Heaven on the Mount of the Olives in Jerusalem. (Marc. 16.19 - Luke 24,51 - Acts 1,9-12). A material proof of the Ascension is the print of Jesus Christ's foot on the rock on top of the Mount of the Olives, visible till our days. So it is the glorious event of

The Mt. of the Olives. In the forground the façade of the Tomb of the Virgin, as restaured by the Crusaders in the XII c. A.D. According to the Apostolic tradition the Holy Virgin was buried by the Apostles in this tomb, which was her family's tomb (St. Ann, St. Joachim and St. Joseph were also buried there), and the third day she ascended to Heaven (Apocryphal Gospel of St. James).

The reliquery which contains the belt of the Holy Virgin. She had trusted it to St. Thomas, as she was ascending to Heaven as testimony that her body did not stay on the earth. The "Holy Belt" is kept in the monastery of Vatopedi at Mt. Athos (Macedonia), - Photo from the book "The wounded Virgin".

the Resurrection that the Apostles transmitted to the pagans, who were living in a decaying world, but who were also expecting salvation.

In fact there are many ancient texts which express this longing, especially the oracles of the Sibyls (pagan prophetesses). The Father of the Church Clemens of Rome, (third bishop of Rome 92-101 A.D.), transmits to us in his work "The Constitutions of the Apostles" the oracle of the Cumaean Sibyl (grotto in Campania of Italy):

> "But when everything turns to dust,
> and when an incorruptible God puts out the fire of life
> which himself lighted up,
> this same God will fashion mankind anew as before.
> And then the judgement will take place
> and the judge will be this God
> and He will judge the world." (Migne P.G.E, VII, 25)
>
> *Translated by the author*
> *from the ancient Greek original*

B. The Christian Face

Evangelisation of Greece 49 A.D.

Among all the pagan nations the Greeks were the first to receive Christianity and later they transmitted the Christian truth to other peoples without using force (as the Roman Catholicism very often did after having changed the Apostolic holy tradition in the XI c. A.D.). Christianity in all its purity of the Orthodox Church is advancing only by teaching, by miracles and by martyrdom. The Hellenic nation was the one most prepared, among all the pagan nations, to receive the Gospel, because of its great philosophers and poets, whose advanced thinking had approached the Evangelical truth in a suprising way. For example Sophocles makes Antigone say: "I was not born to hate, but to love." ("Antigone" 523). Euripides in his tragedy Alcestis" says: "There is nothing more precious in the world, than the human soul." And all the philosophical work of Plato is so much filled with aprehensions of the Truth, that the Father of the Church Clemens of Alexandria in his work "Protreptic" exclaims:" Bravo, Plato, you are touching the Truth! (Migne P.G. 8,49).

As it has already been pointed out, in the ancient world there were "seeds" of the truth, but not all "the Truth", which is based on the Redemption offered by Christ.

Greece was evangelised by St. Paul himself, who arrived in Macedonia (northern Greece) in 49 A.D. He decided to come to Europe from Troas (northern coast of Asia Minor), where he had received a vision: "There stood a man from Macedonia and begged him, saying, Come over to Macedonia and help us". (Acts 16,9). So he sailed from Troas to the island of Samothracea (northern Aegean Sea), and then to the Macedonian coastal town of Neapolis (modern Kavala), at a distance of 9 m. from Philippi, which was situated on the famous Roman road "Egnatia". It is there that he baptised the

61

first Christian of Europe, a woman, and an intelligent one, as she was a business woman: the purple seller Lydia. The little stream where this baptism took place (the first christening in Europe), is still flowing, not far from the Roman forum and the prison of St. Paul mentioned in the XVI ch. of the Acts.

After Philippi St. Paul went to Salonica and then to Berea (western Macedonia), where we see today a magnificent tribune, built at the place where he used to preach. (Acts 16, 10-14). As he was persecuted by the Jews of Macedonia, he sailed in a hurry from the port of Pydna (it does not function today — modern "Touzla Marsh" about 50 km to the south of salonica, close to the national high-way), in order to go to Athens (Acts XVII). After a short stop in this glorious city, where he delivered the famous speech on the "Unknown God", on the Areopagus or Mars Hill at the foot of the Acropolis, he went to Corinth (about 80 km to the west of Athens). There he stayed one year and six months and he founded the first important Christian community of Europe (Acts XVIII). One can visit all these places today by the organized 9 - day tour "In the steps of St. Paul".

In the Roman forum of Ancient Corinth (Agora) we can see today the renowed "Bema", the speakers' platform, where Gallio, the Roman Preconsul and brother of Saneca, tried St. Paul, because of the accusations of the Jews, but Gallio found him not guilty and dismissed him (Acts 18, 12-16). St. Pauls' passage from Corinth is also connected with the ancient harbour of Cenchrea (on the eastern coast of Corinth), where there are remains of an early Christian basilica, built at the point where St. Paul embarked to return to Ephesus (Acts XVIII, 18).

Some other areas of Greece from where St. Paul passed are mentioned in the book of the Acts of the Apostles. For example, Crete, the "Fair Havens" (Acts XXVII, 8) where he left his disciple St. Titus, first bishop of Crete. (His scull is guarded today in the Church of St. Titus in Heraclion-Crete). Rhodes is mentioned also (Acts XXI, I). The place he landed is Lindos, the western natural little harbour, at the foot of the Acropolis, called still "St. Paul's harbour". He also sailed by the island of Lesbos, Chios and Samos (Acts XX, 14-15) and in his Epistle to Titus he mentions that he would spent the winter at Nicopolis (Tit. III, 12) situated near Ac-

Early Christian mosaic (V c. A.D.). Basilica of Doumetios at Nicopolis, western Greece, (near Preveza).

The "Tribune of Gallio" in Corinth, where the trial of St. Paul took place.

The Hellenistic Theatre of Ephesus slightly remodeled by the Romans, where the event mentioned in the XIX ch. of the Acts of the Apostles took place. In this theatre St. Paul would affront wild beasts. ("If after the manner of men I have fought with beasts at Ephesus, what advantageth it me, if the dead rise not?" I. Cor. 15, 32).

The famous basilica of St. John the Evangelist in Ephesus (VI c. A.D.). In the middle of it is the tomb of St. John, who ascended to Heaven after his burial, according to the Apostolic tradition (Apocryphal "Acta Ioannis", Brepols-Turnhout, Belgique, 1983).

tium, in western Greece (near the modern city of Preveza). So Nicopolis became an Apostolic pilgrimage centre in ancient Christian times. That is why we can visit there the early Christian basilicas of the V c. A.D. with magnificent floor mosaïcs, the best in the Balkan peninsula. The XIX ch. of the Acts mentions some events which took place in the ancient theatre of Ephesus, the visit of which is in the programs of the Aegean cruises. (The access is also possible during summer by small boats from the island of Samos. The crossing takes I h.).

To these Christian communities that St. Paul established in Greece, he later sent his famous Epistles: two to the Corinthians, one to the Philippians and two to the Thessalonians. The first Epistle to the Thessalonians is the oldest Christian text, written in Corinth in 52 A.D.).

God sent to Greece some other Apostles too: St. John the Evangelist and "Theologian", also called "the divine", who stayed in exile in the island of Patmos (Dodecanese), in the time of the Roman emperor Domician (81-96 A.D.) Ref. Migne P.G. Irenaeus of Lyon, II c. A.D."Adv. Haer." IV, XX 21, V 35.
Clement of Alexandria (III c. A.D.) "Pedagogue" II, 10, 12 (P. G.).
St. Justin, (II c. A.D.) "Dialogue with Tryphon" (Migne P. G. 81, 4).
Eusebius (IV c. A.D.). In the forword "contra Marcianus" of St. Luke gosp. IV c. A.D.

During this time of his exile in Patmos he received the visions of the "Revelation" (Apocalypse" is in Greek), the last Book of the Holy Bible, direclty from Jesus Christ, the Lord in glory. This miraculous event took place in the sacred cave that we visit during the touristic season by the Aegean cruises. (Access to Patmos is also possible by the liners from Piraeus; the crossing takes 10 h.).

On the right side of the harbour of Patmos (Skala), near the seashore, is situated the original base of the baptistery where St. John the Evangelist christened the pagans of Patmos during his exile. (Narrative of the Deacon Prochorus, an eye witness of these events: Apocrypha "Acta Ioannis", English Ed. by James Rhodes, reprint 1945).

A third Apostle who came to Greece is St. Andrew, the brother of St. Peter. He went to Patras the capital of Achaïa (N.W. of Peloponnese) where he preached the Gospel, made many miracles,

The Holy Cave of the Revelation in Patmos. At the rocky ceiling, on the left, we can see the three fold split which was formed by the earthquake, which took place at the beginning of the Revelation. From this point, which symbolises the Holy Trinity, St. John the Evangelist would hear the voice of God speaking to him".

The little river "Angista" where St. Paul baptised Lydia (first bapti-sm in Europe) - Acts. 16, 12-15.

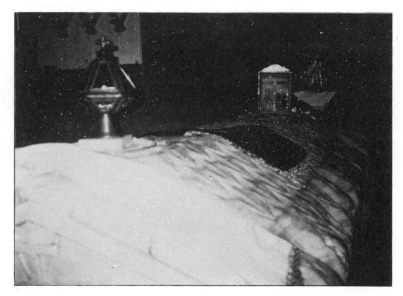

The authentic tomb of St. Luke the Evangelist in Thebes of Beotia. In the church of the old cemetery. (Photo Irene Economides, 1987).

and suffered the martyrdom of crucifixion on a cross in the form of the letter X. In the monumental church in Patras, consacrated to him, his scull and authentic pieces of his cross are to be seen. This church is built near the place of his martyrdom, where a miraculous spring sprung then, and exists till now.

St. Luke the Evangelist who was of Greek origin (Antioch of Syria), came to Thebes (Beotia), where he taught the Gospel, and where he ended his life as a martyr (about 80 A.D.). The authentic tomb of St. Luke the Evangelist (according to the local tradition and the miracles) is situated in the church of the old cemetery of Thebes (XIX c.), built in his memory, (on the right side of the sanctuary). This marble sarcophagus is miraculous although empty, because the holy relics of St. Luke were stolen by the Crusaders during the IV Crusade in 1204 from Constantinople, where they had been transported from Thebes in the IV c. A.D. (Ref. St. Jerome, Father of the Church of the IV c. A.D., in his work "DE VIRIS IL-LUSTRIBUS" in Migne P.L. Ch. 7). The holy relics of St. Luke the Evangelist are today guarded in the Church of St. Justina in Padova of Italy (near Venice).

So the teaching of the Apostles, their miracles and their martyr-dom little by little christianised the pagan world, and the Greek language brought the Gospel to the furthermost limits of the Greco-Roman world, since the original text of the New Testament had been written in Greek. (The Greek language was the universal language of that time and every body could understant it). In this way the prophecy of Jesus Christ, that the Greeks would glorify Him, was fulfiled (John XII, 20-23).

Neverthless this evangelisation of the pagan world did not become possible without sacrifices. For three centuries there was flowing the blood of the martyrs. 11.000.000 is the estimated number of the martyrs in all the Greco-Roman world during the first three centuries of the history of the Church (because of the persecutions of the Roman emperors). 8.000.000 of them were Greeks and a large number among them belonged to the intellectual elit, as is the case of St. Catherine of Alexandria (305 A.D.). At the moment of her martyrdom Angels carried her body to Mt. Sinai, where two centuries later it was discovered by a vision of a hermit. In her memory there was then built her famous monastery on Mt. Sinai, a foundation of the Byzantine Emperor Justinian. This is still functioning, as well as its famous library with precious manuscripts, and the oldest collection of portable icons (VI c. A.D.).

The persecutions stopped by the **Edict of Milan issued by Constantine the Great in 313 A.D.** which granted the Christians freedom of worship. The blood of the martyrs watered the "tree of the Church". The example of holiness and the heroism of the Christians defeated the pagan world which fell like a rotten fruit. Already the Delphic Oracle had given its answer to the messenger of Octavian (the first Roman Emperor), who had asked: "Who will reign after me?": "A Jewish boy will reign, so leave this place in silence". The pagan priests of Delphi had realised that after the great event of the incarnation of God, there was nothing greater to say, so silence would be required as a mark of respect.

A more precise answer of the same Oracle had been given to Julian the Apostate, a successor of Constantine the Great to the throne of Byzantium (361-363 A.D.), who sympathised with the pagans:

"Tell the King, the fairwrought hall has fallen to the ground,
no longer has Phoebus a hut, nor a prophetic laurel,
nor a spring that speaks. The water of speech even is quenched".

Note: This answer is mentioned: a) Philostorgios, "History", book VII, Berlin Ed. pp. 77, 1.18 - Greek text, Latin comment, b) Kedrinos, "History", Ed. Bekker in Germ. vol. I. pp 532. c) Parke and Wormel: "The Delphic Oracle", Ed. Blackwell, Oxford.

This was the last answer of the Oracle of Delphi. Its pagan priests had realised that the exhaustion of paganism was definitive. It was not possible to go backward. A new era was starting and a new civilisation based on the fullness of Truth; the Truth of the universal Saviour, Jesus Christ, "the Son of the Living God".

Half a century before the last answer of the Delphic Oracle, (in 312 A.D.) God had given a direct message to Constantine the Great, as he was marching against his rival Maxentius in Italy. He had seen the cross in the sky "atwart the midday sun" and inscribed with the

St. Themistocles, martyr of the ancient Church (250 A.D.). He was a simple shepherd in the mountains of Lycia (Asia Minor). They cut him up into pieces. His memory: 21 December (contemporary icon by the monk Michael, Mt. Athos).

words: "By this conquer". Immediately Constantine had a standard made bearing the symbol of his vision. It was the first Christian flag. With it in front of his army he was victorious at the battle of the Milvian Bridge (28 Oct. 312 A.D.). Ten years later he defeated his last rival Licinius (in the East, near the Bosphorus, 324 A.D.). This victory left him sole ruler of the East and the West.

Note: About the vision of the cross Ref. Eusebius of Caesaria, "Eccl. History" in Migne P.G., IV c. A.D.).

These events as well as the influence of Constantine's mother, St. Helena, made the Emperor more and more favorable to Christianity. Even the coins of his immense empire had the monogram of Christ.

The Apostolic faith that the martyrs had defended and Constantine favoured, is the Orthodox Christian faith ("Orthodox" means "correct" in Greek). It has come down to us through the successors of the Apostles, in other words the bishops who had been ordained directly by the Apostles (Apostolic succession), such as St. Ignatius, bishop of Antioch and martyr (50-109 A.D.), St. Polycarpus, bishop os Smyrna and martyr (68-155 A.D.), St. Timothy first bishop of Ephesus and martyr, during the reign of Domician (81-96 A.D.). This Orthodox faith has been defended by the Ecumenical Councils against heresies. The first Ecumenical Council was summoned at Nicaea in 325 A.D. (close to the N.E. coast of the Marmora Sea. Today it is called Iznik by the Turks). The Council was under the presidency of Constantine the Great, who as Emperor, wanted to preserve the peace in his State, that was troubled by the heresy of Arianism at that time.

At this council 318 Fathers (Holy bishops of the East and West) established the first 7 articles of the Creed, which has been called the "Nicene Creed". (The last articles were established by the second Ecumenical Council of Constantinople in 381 A.D. defending especially the divinity of the Holy Spirit).

Another important event for the history of Christianity took place in 327 A.D.: the discovery of the Holy Sepulchre and the True Cross and the nails by St. Helena (the mother of Constantine the Great), at Jerusalem. After this discovery, St. Helena built important basilicas in the Holy Land, certain of which still exist (e.g. part of the floor-mosaïc in the basilica of the Nativity in Bethlehem). The largest piece of the True Cross is kept today in the monastery of Xiropotamou on Mt. Athos (Macedonia) and another important piece is at the monastery of St. John the Evangelist and "Theologian" in Patmos (Dodecanese). An authentic nail of the Crucifixion of Christ is to be seen in the church of the Orthodox Patriarchate of Constantinople (on the right side of the wooden iconastasis).

The Byzantine period (330-1453 A.D.)

Constantine the Great was a strategic genious, and realised that ancient Rome was not any more defensible against the pressure of the barbarians. He had also realised that Christianity would be a great help for the power of his Empire and it would be better to have a new capital in the East, where the new religion, as well as the Hellenic culture predominated. So on the 11th of May 330 A.D. he inaugurated the "New Rome" also called Constantinople (city of Constantine), at the same place where the ancient Greek colony Byzantium had been founded by the Greeks of the city of Megara (on the high-way to Corinth), in the VII c. B.C. The leader of these colonizers was called Byzas, and the colony was named after him "Byzantium". In the same way the Empire founded by Constantine the Great has been called the "Byzantine Empire". This was the first Christian empire in the world and its history is part of the history of the Hellenic nation. It is the history of Medieval Greece which lasted over 1.000 years, from the inauguration of the capital city of Constantinople (330 A.D.) till its fall to the Ottoman Turks in 1453.

The geographical position chosen by Constantine for his new capital is the triangular promontory at the entrance of the Bosphorus, on the European coast. It was a tremendously strategic position between two continents; Asia and Europe, and between two seas; the Aegean Sea and the Black Sea. A modern historian has said that "whoever is possessing this point of the Earth, is master of the world". So the Byzantine Empire took an ecumenical character (universal) from the political and the spiritual point of view, as well because of the universality of the Apostolic teaching.

The Byzantine civilisation is a synthesis of the ancient Greek

St. Constantine founder of the Byzantine Empire and his mother St. Helena. The Church called them "equals to the Apostles". Byzantine mosaic, XIII c. A.D., basilica of St. Marc in Venice. - Photo from the "History of the Hellenic Nation" (Vol. VI), publ. Ekdotiki, Athens, 1973.

The Holy Sepulchre in the Church of the Resurrection in Jerusalem, where the miracle of the "Holy Light" takes place every year at the celebration of the Orthodox Easter. On Saturday at the mid-day service all candles and olive oil lamps are out. Suddenly a miraculous light appears at the Tomb of our Lord and lights up the olive-oil lamps and candles of the faithful. This miracle, given by God only to the Orthodox Church, is a proof of the Resurrection of Jesus Christ.

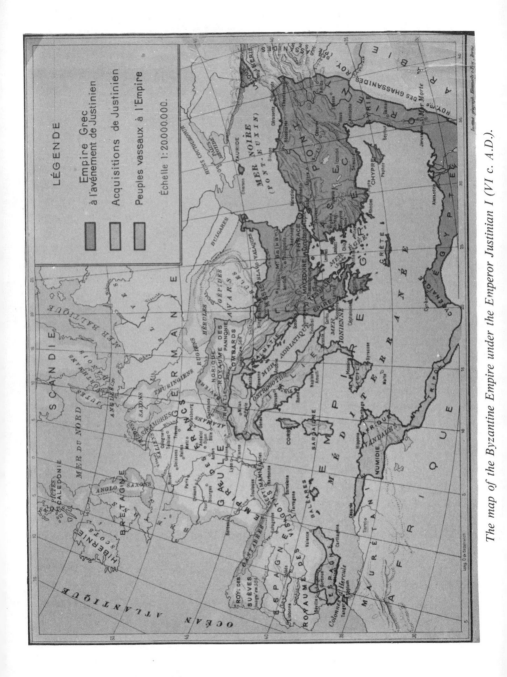

The map of the Byzantine Empire under the Emperor Justinian I (VI c. A.D.).

culture and language, with the spirit of the Roman administration, plus the Christian religion, the Orthodox faith. This is a civilisation of great nobility and fineness, which covered all the brancehs of knowledge, but it excelled especially in theology, hymnography, architecture, painting mosaics, minor arts, music, calligraphy on parchment decorated with miniatures. The monasteries of Byzantium have transmitted to us the ancient Greek literature and science, because a real army of pious copysts for over 1.000 years, were busy copying again and again the ancient manuscripts. This is one of the greatest services of Byzantium to humanity.

Another service that the Byzantine empire rendered to humanity is its successful defence against attacks of barbarian peoples who, had they crossed the empire, would have spread all over Europe. So for 1.100 years Byzantium was the bastion of Christian Europe. A proof of this is that the pressure of the Arab world in the VII c. A.D. took the direction along northern Africa towards Spain and sounth France, because they had failed to get through the Empire.

During the millenium of its life the Byzantine Empire had ups and downs, according to the capacities and the personality of its Emperors. During the periods of the greatest power and expansion (VI c. under the Emperor Justinian I and XI c. under the Macedonian dynasty) the eastern border of the Empire was the river Euphrates in Mesopotamia, the northern border was the river Danube and the southern coast of Crimea, the western border was Italy as far as Milan and certain coasts of southern Spain, the southern border was the coast of northern Africa, all Asia Minor and the Middle East as far as the eastern coast of the Black Sea.

During this millenium three artistic Renaissances took place after the early Christian Art that had flourished under Constantine the Great and Theodossius in the IV c. A.D.

The first Renaissance took place in the VI c. in the reign of the Emperor Justinian (527-565 A.D,) who built splendid churches, such as St. Sophia of Constantinople, the cathedral of the Byzantine capital. It was dedicated to Jesus Christ, the incarnate Wisdom of God (Sophia: Wisdom), and it is symbol of Christian Hellenism. The renowed churches (because of their mosaics) of Ravena in Italy, and the Monastery of St. Catherine on Mt. Sinai, with mosaics and icons of the VI c. A.D. belong to Justinian's building program. From the basilicas of northern Africa and Palestine there exist today only floor-mosaics (except the colonade of redish marble of the basilica of the Nativity in Bethlehem). Another important monument of this period is the basilica of St. John the Evangelist in Ephesus, which was preserved intact till the XV c. when it was destroyed by Tamerlan. This church was one of the greatest pilgrimages of Christendom, built at the place of the Assumption of St. John (celebrated on 26 of September). One should also mention the pearl of the Aegean: the "Ecatondapyliani" church of Paros (Cyclades).

The second Renaissance under the Macedonian dynasty in the XI c. gave great monuments with mosaic decoration such as the monastery of Hossios Loukas in Phokis (area of Delphi), dedicated to the saint and hermit Hossios Loukas (IX - X c. A.D.). His relics are now in his monastery having been transportde from Venice recently. Antother famous monastery of this period is the monastery of Daphni, near Athens, the mosaics of which desplay a Hellenistic elegance, which proves that the Byzantine art is not rigid, but it follows different tendencies and finally leads to a marvelous synthesis. A third monastery decorated with mosaics of an astonishing quality (XI c.) is "Nea Moni" in the island of Chio. St. Sophia of Monemvasia (south Peloponese) is also worth mentioning. A douzen of chapels in the area of Athens are charming, as well as the small churches of Kastoria (western Macedonia) and those of Cappadocia (in the caves).

In the XII c. this renaissance continued and produced the masterpieces of St. Marc's mosaics in Venice, and those of Monreal Church, near Palermo in Sicily, as well as the dilightful chapel of the Holy Virgin in the Monastery of St. John the Envagelist and "Theologian" in the island of Patmos.

The third Renaissance took place after the end of the Frankish occupation of Byzantium during the IV Crusade (1204), one of the most shameful events of the universal history. (The plundering of the Crusaders in the Byzantine capital was awful: they stole the treasures, the precious manuscripts and important relics of saints. Their fury was such, that they detached the precious stones of St Sophias holy table by means of iron tools. All these precious and

The Emperor Justinian I (527-565 A.D.). Great general and legislator. He created the Corpus juris civilis Justiniani which was in use in western Europe since the XII c. untill very recently. The Empress Theodora reigned with him. Mosaic of the VI c. A.D., St. Vital in Ravenna. Photo from the "History of the Hellenic Nation", publ. Ekdotiki, Athens, 1973.

The cupola of St. Sophia in Constantinople, VI c. A.D. It is supported by two semi-cupolas on the eastern and the western side and by four pendentives decorated with cherubims. The hight of this cupola is of 55,60 m. and the average diameter 31,87 m. The light through 40 windows arround the cupola gives the impression that we are standing under Heaven. The architects of St. Sophia were Greeks from Asia Minor: Anthemius of Tralles and Isidorus of Miletus.

holy things are to be seen today in museums, libraries and churches of the West).

Constantinople stayed under the Crusaders for almost 60 years, till 1261, when she was liberated again by the Greeks. In other areas of the Empire the Franks stayed longer. For example in Peloponnese and in the islands, where they built many fortresses.

The reason of the Frankish domination of the Byzantine Empire was the wealth of the Byzantine capital, which was the most beautiful and the wealthiest city of the world in those days. Constantinople was called: "the Queen City". But the pretext for the attack was the dogmatic separation after the Great Schism (1.054 A.D.), following the dogmatic reformation in the West by Charlemagne in 809 A.D. (He deformed the article of the Nicene Creed about the Holy Spirit - addition of the "Filioque"). The western Europeans who were responsible for the reformations (another reformation was the "Juridical Primacy" of the bishop of Rome, which started in the IX c. under pope Nicolas I 858-867 A.D.), considered the Christians of Byzantium, who defended the Holy Apostolic Faith, as enemies. Humanity is still living the consequences of the IV Crusade, because the Byzantine Empire never recovered the power that it had possessed before, and the approaching Turks, who were advancing gradually from Turkestan westwards, found the opportunity to conquer it.

Note: On this subject consult the book of the same author: "Differences between the Orthodox Church and Roman Catholicism". (Orders: "Philocalia" bookstore: 38, Voulis str. Athens 105.57, Tel. 323.4411).

The third Renaissance (XIV c.) is very moving, because it proves that Hellenism, even after the trial of the Frankish occupation, that had so much weakened the nation, was able again to create something new and even very beautiful. This last Byzantine Renaissance, which is called "the Art of the Paleologues" (last Byzantine dynasty), is of great refinement and elegance and it is approaching the classical ideal of ancient Greece (architecture, painting, mosaics, miniatures, hymnography). The monuments of this period which we can admire today are the churches of Mystra (near Sparta), the churches of Athos and of the Balkan countries

The defensive walls of Constantinople, IV & V c. A.D. as they are today. They repelled Barbarian attacks during a millenium. There were land walls and sea walls. The entrance to the bay of the Golden Horn was defended by a huge bronze chain. Some pieces of it are to be seen in the Maritime Museum of Constantinople. (Photo from the "History of the Hellenic Nation", vol VII, publ. Ekdotiki, Athens 1973.

(where Greek artists had worked), the churches of Salonica (Macedonia), the famous church of Chora (Cariye museum) in Constantinople, decorated with the best preserved and finest mosaics of the Byzantine Art, as well as the lovely chapels of Crete.

Neverthless the Byzantine Empire had shrunk in size. The Turks had already occupied Asia Minor in the XIV c. and in April 1453 they were in front of the walls of Constantinople. These famous walls of the IV and V c. A.D. which during 1.000 years had resisted all the barbarian attacks, finally fell to the hands of the Turks by betrayal, in spite of the heroic resistance of several weeks (6 April - 29 May 1453) to a terrible siege.

A three-day looting and slaughtering (promised by Mohamet the Conqueror to his soldiers) followed and the church of St Sophia, as all the important churches of Greece became mosques.

This was the new "Thermopylae" of the Hellenic nation, where the last Emperor of Byzantium, Constantine Paleologue, fell as a simple soldier defending his fatherland, as a new Leonidas, against a much more powerful enemy; the defenders of the city were 5.000 Greeks and 2.000 foreign merceneries, and the regular Turkish army had 80.000 soldiers apart from the Asiatic hordes following the army.

The last mass in Santa Sophia

God rings the bells, the eath rings the bells,
and Santa Sophia, the great church, rings the bells:
a priest for each bell and a deacon for each priest.
To the left the Emperor was chanting, to the right the Patriarch,
and from the volume of the chant the pillars were shaking.
When they were about to sing the hymn of the Cherubims,
they hear a voice from Heaven and from the mouth of the
Archangel:
"Stop the cherubic hymn, and let the Holy elements bow in mourn-
ing.
You, the priests, take the holy vessels and you candles must be ex-
tinguished,
for it is the will of god that the city fall to the Turks.
But send a message to the West asking for three ships to come;
one to take the Cross away, another the Holy Bible,
the third, the best of them, our Holy Altar,
lest the dogs size it from us and defile it".
The Virgin was destressed, and the holy icons wept.
"Hush, Lady" do not weep so profusely,
after years and after centuries, they will be yours again".

Greek folk song
Transl. by Const. Trypanis

TROPAIRE

Verbe co-é-ter-nel au Père et à l'Es-prit, toi qui es né de
la Vier-ge pour no-tre sa-lut, nous te chan-tons, nous tes fi-dè-les, et
t'a-do-rons, Sei-gneur, car tu as bien vou-lu souf-frir en mon-tant
sur la croix pour y su-bir la mort en ta chair et res-sus-ci-ter les
morts en ta sainte et glo-ri-eu-se Ré-sur-rec-tion.

*Byzantine hymn which glorifies the Resurrection of the Lord., publ.
Monastery of Chevetogne, Harvesin, Belgium.*

Example 27.
Athens MS. 2406 fol. 464r.

A piece of Byzantine music: The hymn of the Cherubims, used during the liturgy (Sunday service). "Byzantine Cherubika" of the XIV & XV c., Patriarchal Institute of Patristic Studies, Salonica, 1974.

86

Mosaic in Byzantine style (IX c. A.D.), Abbey at Germigny-des-Prés (near Orleans) in France. This is a proof of the Byzantine influence in the West.

The Angels are protecting the Arch of the Covenant. In the middle, ver-tically, is the hand of God.

Whoever studies the Byzantine history and civilisation objectively, feels a profound respect for these Christian Greeks, who, being obliged to fight constantly for their freedom, against all kinds of uncivilised peoples, succeeded, at the same time, in civilising many nations, and in creating the finest and noblest civilisation, the civilisation of the "sublime". The Greek professor at the School of Fine Arts in Athens, P. Michelis, in his work "the Esthetics of Byzantine Art", said: "If ancient Greece expressed the "beautiful", Byzantine Greece expressed the "sublime".

The means that the Greeks of Byzantium used in order to accomplish their civilising role, were the Orthodox missions, the diplomacy which was very skilled, and the dispatch of their princesses as wives to the Kings of the East and the West.

This civilisation of the "sublime" has bequethed to us an invaluable treasure: the works of the Greek Fathers which cover a period of 15 centuries: "the Patristic". A gigantic accomplishment of the human spirit, which is not only theoretical, but also practical, because these authors were also great saints, and true ascetics, who lived the evangelical truths in their personal lives. This is why today they are increasingly translated in all European languages, and so much read by the larger public (Paper-back editions).

The influence of Byzantium in Western Europe was enormous in all the fields. So it is not without reason that the famous Belgian Byzantinologist H. Gregoire shouted in the IX International Congress of Byzantine Studies (Salonica 12-25 April 1953): "Long live Byzantine Europe. Long Live Byzantine Greece!"

The Byzantine civilisation belongs to Europe. It has been proved by the science of History and by the famous International Exhibition which took place in Athens in 1964, under the title: "Byzantine Art - European Art" (Catalogue on sale at the Byzantine Museum in Athens). But according to the same Byzantinologist H. Gregoire, "The natural and lawful heirs of Byzantium are the Greeks".

So the Turkish attack stopped the evolution of the European civilisation by enslaving its most dynamic element: Hellenism.

Notes: One of the most famous Orthodox missions was that of the two Greek brothers from Salonica: St. Methodius and St. Cyril, who were monks of high education. They had been sent to Moravia (modern Czechoslovakia), at the invitation of the King of that country (IX c. A.D.), in order to bring there the Gospel, the alphabet and the civilisation. Since then the alphabet of the Slavs is called "Cyrilic", because it was created by St. Cyril. As he was a Greek he adapted the Greek alphabet to the Slavonic language. Their disciples continued the evangelisation of Central and Eastern Europe. The Russian people also received Orthodoxy from the Greeks of Byzantium in the X c. A.D. after the invitation of the Prince of Kiev who became St. Vladimir.

b) Many Greek princesses of the Byzantine court were married to foreign rulers, introducing thus the Byzantine civilisation to their new homes. From this list we shall present only two important cases: Princess Theophano, niece of the Byzantine emperor Tzimisces, became the wife of the German King Otto II (955-983), and introduced the Greek classical studies to the German court. Princess Ann "prophyrogenete" (born in the purple") was sent to Russia in 988 as wife of the Prince of Kiev Vladimir, first Orthodox King of Russia, and who worked for the evangelisation of her new country.

The period of the Turkish domination (1453-1821)

Greece suffered terribly during the four centuries under the rule of a tyrannic and barbarous conqueror.

a) The taxes were very heavy for the Christians (heavier than those for the Moslems). Very often those who were weak in faith were islamized voluntarily in order to avoid overtaxing.

b) The administration was arbitrary. There was no justice. The Greeks could not defend either their family, or their property, or their faith, or honour.

c) Beautiful women were forcibly conducted to the harems or to the slave markets. The most clever and the most healthy boys were abducted by thousands and turned into Janissaries (the most cruel Turkish soldiers) and islamized by force. Some were brought up to serve as future high-officers of the Ottoman Empire).

d) The barbarous conqueror had prohibited the function of schools. So the monasteries became centres of moral resistance for the nation, by running secret schools. To these evening classes in churches and monasteries only boys could go in the night, often in danger of their lives as they had to cross mountains and forests in order to get there and learn how to read and write their language. As books, they had only the liturgical books of the

The renowed monastery of the Holy Virgin "Proussiotissa", where there is kept a miraculous icon 1.300 years old. One of the secret schools was functioning here in the XVIII c. (central Greece to the west of Lamia, via Carpenission).

Church, and as teachers humble and heroic monks. A folk song of that period is the following:

> "Little bright moon,
> light my way to school;
> so as to learn how to read
> godly things".
>
> *(Translated by the author)*

Some of these secret schools can be visited today. One situated on the outskirts of Athens, in the monastery of the Holy Virgin (XVI c.) on Mt. Pendelikon, by the high-way (10 m). Another one is situated on the little island of the Ioannina lake (capital of Epirus-N.W of Greece). This is the monastery of Philanthropinon, where, in the narthex, we can see Greek philosophers painted on the walls besides the saints of the Church!

In the record of this painful education we must not omit a young woman who, in the XVI c. (the darkest period in Greece) had the courage to establish in Athens the first school in the world for young girls, providing both the money and the labour. She also created professional workshops in her house, transformed into a nunnery, in order to help poor girls to earn their living and save them from the harem. She is St. Philothea the Athenian, a member of a noble family, who became a nun and martyr. She was killed by the Turks in a northern suburb of Athens, which bears her name. Her precious relics are guarded and venerated at the Metropolitan Church of Athens (near Constitution sq.). Her memory is on the 19 February.

e) During the four centuries of the Turkish occupation countless revolutions took place, because the Greeks had never accepted slavery, but all these revolutions finished in slaughters.

f) Apart from mass-slaughterings, there were in Greece, during these four centuries 35.000 new martyrs of Christianity. They were those who had to answer the dilemma, either to die as Christians, or turn into Moslems. (In spite of the initial law of Mohamet II the Conqueror, who had said that the faith of the occupied nations should be respected).

Traditional Architecture (XVIII c.) in the villages of Mt. Pelion (eastern Thessaly), in which we distinguish the survival of the civil architecture of the Byzantine period.

Wood-carving from a mansion of Kozani, XVIII c. (western Macedonia), presently in the Benaki Museum. (Photo of the guide-book 1980).

Some brave Greeks who did not like to live under this awful rule, went to the mountains as partisans. Those were the famous "Klephtes" (the thieves) who later on formed the army of the War of Independence. They were men of great heroism and great virtue, able to fight for days without bread or water, and had no physicians to tend their wounds. But during the hours of leisure they would sing of their exploits and they danced the wariors' dance (Tsamikos).

The folk songs and dances of Modern Greece continue the tradition of ancient and Byzantine Greece, and with the other branches of the folk-lore such as the regional costumes, the embroideries, the decorative arts (ceramic, wood-carving, silver-ware, jewels) as well as the survival of the language, constitute the best proof-that the same people continues to live in this country. (Benaki Museum - Folk Museum in Plaka, 17, Kydathynaion st. - cassetts and records of the old folk music - Dora Stratou "Folk dance theatre" at the foot of Philopappos hill, opposite the Acropolis).

Hellenism has been able to keep itself alive in the middle of all these sufferings, keep up its ideals, and especially the national feeling and the Orthodox Christian faith, this great mobilising power, which helped the nation to regain its liberty. Certain great saints, mostly monks of Mt. Athos, had prepared the Greek people for the great event of the Independence. Two of them are St. Nicodemus the Agiorite, (monk of Mt. Athos), who, in his humble cell, wrote patristic texts in simplified Greek, and St. Cosmas the Aitolian, who crossed almost all Greece on foot, teaching the villagers in the open air and fostering faith (XVIII c.) He finished his life as a martyr, hung by the Turks.

There were also a few schools of higher education in certain privileged areas (Mt. Athos, Patmos, Trebizond, Constantinople), which prepared the future spiritual leaders and organizers of the revolutionary movement. ("The Friendly Association": Philiki Eteria). The statue of one of the three founders of this Association, Emmanuel Xanthos, is to be seen at the harbour of the island of Patmos.

A Hellenic institution known already in antiquity, and which flourished again towards the end of the Byzantine period (XIII-XV c.), is found again during the Turkish occupation; this is the democratic administration and the communal organization of the economy. There are documents of the local legislation of Myconos, the Statute of the co-operative of "Ambelakia" in Thessaly (on the slopes of Mt. Ossa to the east of Mt. Olympus), the communal system of Hydra's commercial fleet, as well as those of certain villages in Epirus, which prove that it was not the French Revolution that inspired the Greek revolt; on the contrary, the democratic and communal feeling had never stopped inspiring the Greeks, all the more as the democratic spirit governs the Orthodox Church (Synodical System). So the democratic and community system of occupied Hellenism was one of the decisive factors that made the War of Independence successful.

The Hellenic nation also showed another kind of grandeur during this cruel period: the virtue of patience in sufferings, the heroism of holiness and perseverance in tortures. We know from the Gospel that patience and humility bring divine help and Grace. The Greek people has lived in all the plenitude of this Grace during his long penitence, because of some excessive sins in the Byzantine period (this was the general feeling of the nation and of its spiritual leaders). Since 1453 till 1821 ten Ecumenical Patriarchs finished their lives as martyrs, dozens of bishops, and thousands of priests and monks. All together 6.000.

A painting representing the oath of the Greek warriors at the Monastery of St. Lavra, in the presence of the bishop of Patras Guermanos, on 25th of March 1821. This date is the national festival of Greece. This monastery is located near the village Calavryta (northern Peloponnese). Photo from the Guidebook of Benaki Museum, 1980.

The period of the War of Independence (1821-1828)

"An eagle wet and snowed
pleads the sun to rise:
Do rise, Sun!"

Greek folk song
translated by the author.

The war of Independence broke out it March 1821 in Peloponnese, the year of Napoleon's death in Santa Helena. This is not a simple coincidence! When Napoleon, who wanted to unite Europe by the force of weapons died, Greece, she, who is going to unite Europe by the power of the Spirit, began to revive.

The general of the War of Independence Theodore Kolokotronis said: "We took up the arms for the holy faith of Christ, and for the liberty of our fatherland. "This war, unique in the world's history, is a war of a people, who, bare-footed, without sufficient means, without an organized army, defeated a barbarian and powerful conqueror, whom even the great Powers of the West respected. The Sultan was completely ridiculed.

This war started at "Tainaron", the southernmost promontory of continental Europe, as the decisive uprise took place in the city of Areopolis (south of Sparta) on 17 March 1821, sparkling nationalism in many European countries, such as Italy and Germany.

All the Hellenic nation took part in this desperate war: from Northern Epirus (modern southern Albania), a Greek province from antiquity, with ancient Greek monuments and Byzantine churches, and where 400.000 Greeks, Orthodox Christians, are suffering persecutions because of their faith (100.000 Greek Orthodox are in concentration camps and 25.000 in prison under a totalitarian regime (the most atheistic in the world), as far as Cyprus, which has also been Greek province since at least the second millenium B.C. and where they still speak and write the Greek language. (Slabs of the "Linear B" script have been discovered in Cyprus as in Peloponnese and in Crete), not to mention the ancient and Byzantine monuments which demonstrate Cyprus' Greek character. The different occupations of this island; Arab, Frankish, Turkish, British, have not

Ερείπια ἀρχαίου ναοῦ εἰς τήν Ἀ-
πολλωνίαν, κοντά εἰς τήν σημερινήν
Αὐλώνα τῆς Βορείου Ἠπείρου.

Ancient Greek temple in Northern Epirus (south Albania), from the ancient town Apollonia, near modern Avlona.

changed its national identity. 500.000 Greeks were living in Cyprus till 1974, the Turkish minority was 18% — when the illegal Turkish attack changed the population of the northern part of the island (since then they have occupied 40% of the Cypriot territory, part of an independend country and member of the United Nations). The Turks transferred there populations from the interior of Turkey, and expelled the Greek-Cypriots to the southern part of the island, where they have lived since then as refugies (200.000), having lost all their property, in spite of the resolutions of the United Nations and the International Law. Since 1974 Turkey has ridiculed the International Organisations and the Alliance of N.A.T.O. The principle of "self-determination" of the U.N. conceived for the liberation of the colonies after the Second World War, has been trangressed in Cyprus, as the referendum of the Greek - Cypriots of 1950 (98% voted for "union with Greece") has never been respected.

What is happening today in Cyprus and in Albania is a slap against western civilisation and the protective Powers. Moreover instead of driving out from the International Organisation these two countries, which do not respect the principles of the Charter of U.N. they have granted the presidency of the Council of Europe to Turkey, whose only European possession is Oriental Thrace, another Greek province, from where the Greek population was uprooted by force during the First World War.

If Northern Epirus and Cyprus were not Greek provinces with a Greek population possessing the Hellenic national consciousness, these areas would not have participated in the Greek War of Independence. Neverthless both of them participated and with great heroism. The Archbishop of Cyprus Cyprian was hung by the Turks, when the revolt broke out there. As he was dying he sang: "If the world is going to perish, Greece will be the last to perish".

Many distinguished members of the Orthodox clergy gave their lives for Greece during the War of Independence. Not only bishops, but also simple priests and humble monks, suffering terrible tortures, or by participating in the battles. But the martyrdom which mostly moved the Hellenic nation was that of the Ecumenical Patriarch of Constantinople Gregory V, who was hung in front of the Patriarchate's door (which since then remains closed). This happened on 10 April 1821, on Easter day. The body of the Patriarch

101

The marble forum of Ancient Salamis in Cyprus, Greek colony founded by the brother of Ajax, King of the island of Salamis and hero of the Trojan War.

Near this rock, at the southern coast of Cyprus (on the way to Paphos), Aphrodite was born, according to the Greek Mythology. That is why Aphrodity was also called "Cyprian". (Aphrodite means born from the foam).

was thrown in the Bosphorus and a Greek captain from Kefallinia, saw the body in the night near his ship, and transported it to Odessa (Krimaia), where it was burried and where it remained till 1871.

Gregory V has been canonized, his relics are today kept at the Metropolitan Church of Athens, and his statue stands in front of the Athens University. The simple coffin in which the captain transported the body to Odessa, is now in the island Kefallinia (western Greece), in a chapel of the village Domata. The Patriarch's cross of blessing is now in the museum of St. John's the Evangelist Monastery in Patmos. His episcopal staff in the Byzantine Museum in Athens and his miter in the monastery of Prophet Elijah in Santorini.

The motto of the revolted Greeks was: "Freedom or death". All the Greek people: men, women, children, elderly men and women made their contribution with a heroism much greater thar that of the Trojan War or of the Persian Wars.

Neverthless European diplomacy was not favorable towards this revolution, which was shaking the "Status Quo" after the Napoleonic Wars. So the Greek people was struggling alone, except a philhellenic movement which became stronger after Lord Byron's death, who gave his life for Greece at Missolonghi in 1824 (southwestern Greece).

Young Europeans who had studied classics decided to come as volonteers and fight for the Greek cause. They came from different countries of Europe: France, Italy, England, even from Finland and two American Doctors from the United States. In the small Roman Catholic Chapel of Nauplia (in the old mosque of the upper town), one can see the list of the European Philhellens, who gave their life for Greece on the battlefields. In the middle of the square at the harbour of the same town we can see the marble monument commemorating the French Philhellenes. In the historical park of Missolonghi there are many monuments in their honour. The intellectual elite of Europe began to awake after the glorious victories of the Greeks, and mass slaughterings. The Italian poet Santore di Santaroza gave his life for Greecs. (His tomb is on the coast of the island of Sphaktiria in Pylos, S.W. of Peloponnese). The French poet Victor Hugo wrote the poem "The Greek child" in his "Orientales", and the French painter Eg. Delacroix made many paintings inspired by

Fresco of Christ "Pantocrator" (the All-Mighty), at the cupola of Assinou Church (Mt. Troodos in Cyprus), XIV c.

Lord Byron in a souliot costum (mountainous area of Epirus celebrated for the heroism of its men and women). Lord Byron wrote once: "It is Greece that made me a poet". Painting, Benaki Museum, Athens.

Greek warrior. National Historical Museum. This costume was wore by Greek men till King Otho's reign. This costume is called "evzone", which means elegant waist. The Greek army wore the "evzone" uniform till the I World War and one regiment till the II World. Today only the National guard wears it and some elderly men in mountain villages.

MISS MADON
(DAUGHTER of the HOSPODAR, NICHOLAS MAVROGUENI)
The DISTINGUISHED HEROINE from MICONO
a small Island in the Grecian Archipelago

Drawn from Life & Published in London, April 1825, by A. Fraikel,
& sold by all the Principal Printsellers

Mando Mayroguenous, one of the great heroines of the Greek Independence, of a noble family of the island of Paros. She armed two warships on her own budget and she took part at naval battles and at the siege of Karystos (south Eubea). Her statue is at the central square of Myconos. On the island of Paros we can see her house, where she finished her life in poverty in 1848. Photo: Folk Museum of Myconos.

The flagship of Miaoulis, the Greek admiral of the War of Independence. The role of the merchant-marine was very important for the liberation of Greece. The flag with white and blew stripes is the flag of the Hellenic navy till the present day. Painting at the Benaki Museum.

these events. The most famous of them is the "Massacre of Chios" (copies are to be seen in the National Historical Museum in Athens, and in the War Museum).

Ships of the English, the French and Russian fleets took part in the events, although their orders were not to interfer. This is the famous naval battle of Navarino, near ancient Pylos (S.W. of Peloponnese), on 20 October 1827. The Egyptian fleet under the command of Ibrahim Pasha (ally of the Turks) was completely destroyed by the united European fleet and today its fragments lie at the bottom of Navarino's bay. In the middle of the square of Modern Pylos one can see a monument in honour of the three European Admirals: the British Sir Edward Condrighton, the French de Rigny, and the commander of the Russian fleet the Duch Admiral Heiden. Arround the bay we can see the monuments in honour of the European sailors who were killed at this battle for the liberty of Greece.

Three years after this decisive battle the Great Powers of Europe signed the Independence of Greece as Guarantee Powers, in London (1830), and the first few verses of the "Hymn to Liberty" of the national Greek poet Dion. Solomos (1798-1857) became the national Anthem of Greece.

The poet is addressing the personified Liberty saying;

"I recognize you by the fierce edge of your sword;
I recognize you by the look that measures the earth.
Liberty, who sprang out of the sacred bones of the Greeks,
brave as in the past, I greet you, I greet you!"

Trans. by Const. Trypanis

A great friend of Greece, who had seen her before the Revolution, on his way to the Holy Land, was Chateaubriand. In his book "Itenerary to Jerusalem" he included essays on Greece such as the "Sunrise on the Acropolis". Thinking about the Greek civilisation he wrote:

"Greece!
A name that we cannot pronounce
without respect and emotion".

These words are engraved on the base of his statue that Greece, grateful, erected in his honour (King Constantine Ave. — Hilton area Athens).

110

Greece among the ruins of Missolonghi. Painting of the French artist Eugène Delacroix, 1826.

The first governor of Independend Greece, count John Capodistria. (1828-1831). Before he became the Governor of Greece, when he still was Secretary of State of Imperial Russia, he had been the creator of the political uninity and the constitution of Switzerland. His diplomatic skill helped also France at the tragic moment of the desaster following Napoleon's defeat. (Recent historical ressearch of Mrs Helen Koukkou, professor of History at the University in Athens).

The Period of Independent Greece (1830)

"This soil is a sacred oratory.
It will not be trodden by barbarian foot,
unless it perishes for ever."

Dion. Solomos
translated by the author.

As the three powers which signed the Independence of Greece were monarchies; Great Britain, France under Charles X, and Imperial Russia, Greece also became a Kingdom with a foreign King: Otho, prince of Bavaria (1833-1862).

King Otho landed at Nauplia less than 20 years old, escorted by three Bavarian regents, after the assassination of the first Governor of Independent Greece: count John Capodistria, who originated from the island of Corfu (western Greece), where there is his tomb today (Monastery of the Holy Virgin "Platytera"). Count Capodistria had given up his post as Secretary of State in Imperial Russia, in order to come and work in Greece. He did so unpaid and offering his property to the impoverished country in order to help it to come out of the chaos. He was assassinated by a Greek, who was not pleased by the way of his government, and who was pushed to it by the British diplomacy, because of the British interests in the Mediterranean (this was acknowledged by the murderer). To the right of the entrance of St. Spyridon church, in the old section of the city, one can see the marks left by the murderer's bullets. Some personal objects of the Governor are today exhibited at the Benaki Museum in Athens and the National Historical Museum.

His government was very wise, based on the traditions of the country; and the Treaty of Adrianople (1829) and the Protocol of London (1830) which granted complete independence to Greece were due to his diplomatic skill. If Greece did not have the misfortune to lose so early such a man (also martyr), she would have developped in a more normal way, without the political troubles which followed later and without losing the compass of her true orientation. (The statue of the first Governor of Independent Greece is to be seen at the central square of Nauplia (eastern Peloponnese).

In fact the accession to the throne of Greece of a foreign King changed the spiritual orientation of the country, which, since then, has been under the influence of foreign interests. It is enough to know that the first three political parties of Modern Greece were called: "the British party", the French Party" and "the Russian party"! The strategic situation of Greece in the Mediterranean is such, that the Great Powers never left Greece on its own. Only some great statesmen managed to steer the country through the political intrigues of the Great Powers to our national interests.

There are three museums in Athens where one can study the history of Independent Greece: the National Historical Museum, the Benaki Museum, and the War Museum.

The Absolute Monarchy (1833-1862)

King Otho (who was a Roman Catholic, while Queen Amalia a Protestant) after the date of his majority he governed Greece as an absolute monarch, without respecting the democratic character of the Greeks. He also interfered in religious matters by transgressing the canons of the Orthodox Church on the election of the bishops (who must be elected by the faithful: clergy and lay-people: the people of God on Earth), by closing hundreds of monasteries, under the pretext of the small number of monks or nuns in them, and confiscating their property and ecclesiastical treasures dictatorilly. He did not hesitate to detach the Church from the Ecumenical Patriarchate of Constantinople and create the "Autocephalus Church of Greece" (autocephalus: self-governing), in order to be able to manipulate the churche's affairs! Greece still pays for the consequences of these measures. The Greek people, very dissatisfied, revolted in 1843 demanding a constitution. They gathered in front of his palace (now the Parliament), and fortunately the demonstration ended without bloodshed. Otho was obliged to grant the constitution, but he never respected it. He was finally deposed in 1862. He returned to Bavaria with Queen Amalia, without having established a dynasty, as he had no descendants. In the Benaki Museum are exhibited the penholder with which the Contitution was signed, as well as the portrait ot the King and the Queen, and the two famous armchairs, transported from the island of Hydra to Nauplia for the

114

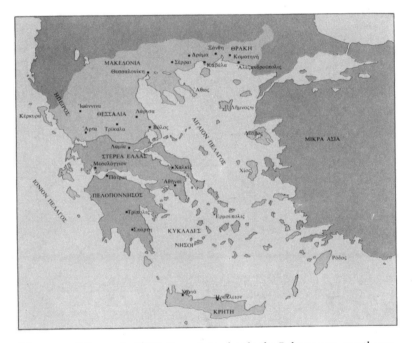

The map of Greece in 1830. It contained only the Peloponnese, south continental Greece, the island Eubea and the Cyclades. Central and northern
Greece, as well as the big islands of the Aegean Sea stayed under Turkish
rule according to the arbitary decision of the three protective European
powers. The population of this small state was 700.000 inh.

welcome of Otho and the Regent on his arrival in Greece in 1833. In the Museum of the "City of Athens" we can see an original drawing-room of his palace.

King Otho influenced by his studies of classical Greece had not understood the role of the medieval Byzantine empire, so all the educational program for the young Greeks was based on a cold classicism, having no relation with the Byzantine tradition. The wealthy families used to send their sons to Germany for higher studies, so all the intellectual elite of the XIX c. Greece was influenced by western" "Positivisme". A great saint of this period, known as monk "Papoulakos" organized a moral resistance, which has had a certain influence on the people, especially in Peloponnese, but he was put in prison. Other intellectual persoralities were persecuted by this regime as well.

The Period of Constitutional Monarchy (1863-1924)

By conscent of Great Britain (one of the three protecting powers) another foreign King arrived in Greece: a Danish prince who became George the Ist of Greece (1863-1913). He brought as a gift, by courtesy of Britain, the liberty of the Ionian islands (western Greece), which had been a British Protectorate after the Napoleonic Wars. We must know that the Protecting Powers had not permitted Greece to have its normal border, in spite of the fact that all the nation had stuggled heroicaly from the North to the South. So Greece's border from 1830 to 1863 was to the North Mt. Othrys (near Lamia), and from the islands it possessed only Eubea and the Cyclades. This was a great injustice, justified only by the European diplomacy that respected the Sultan too much!

George Ist was the only King of contemporary Greece truly constitutional, this is why his reign was rather happy and very long (50 years). He had the happiness to see Greece larger after the Treaty of Berlin (1878) which granted Thessaly (central part of the country) and the southernmost part of Epirus. (These provinces were finally annexed to Greece in 1881). He also saw the liberation of a part of northern Greece and Salonica (1912), where he was assassinated on 5 March 1913, by an enemy of Greece, reputedly from one of the Balkan countries.

The Queen-Mother Olga with her grand-daughters. (Photo: 1 January 1921). Standing from left to right:
1. Elizabeth, later Countess of Terring. 2. Xenia, later Mrs Leeds, 3. Olga, later wife of Paul of Yougoslavia. 4. Theodora, later Grand Duchess of Baden. 5. Nina, daughter of the Grand-Duchess Maria. 6. Margaret, later princess Hohenlohe.
Seating: 7. Cecil, later Grand-Duchess of Essen. 8. Irene, daughter of King Constantine, later Duchess of Aoste. 9. Helen, daughter of King Constantine, later Queen - Mother of Rumania.
Seating on the floor: Cathreen, daughter of King Constantine, later Mrs Brandram. 11 Sophia, later princess of Hannover (wife of Ernest). 12. Marina, later Duches of Kent. (Photo of Serpieris Collection from the book "Contemporary History of Greece", by Sp. Markezinis, vol. (1920-1936), Publ. Papyros, 1973.

George Ist married the archduchess Olga of Russia who gave him many children. The crown prince was Constantine (period of the Ist World War), who married the Kaïzer's sister, princess Sophia. This marriage created many problems to Greece during this troubled period, because the official policy of Greece under its renowed Prime Minister El. Venizelos was the cooperation with the Western Alliance (Britain-France-Italy), while the King sympathised with the Germans.

Eleftherios Venizelos was from Crete; he was one of the greatest diplomatic personalities of Modern Europe and the greatest statesman of contemporary Greece. Under his government Greece almost tripled in size with the aquisition of Macedonia, Epirus, and Thrace in the Balcan Wars 1912-1913. As a result of these great victories against the Turks, the islands of the Aegean Sea were annexed to Grece: Crete, Lesbos, Chios and Samos. (Commander-in-Chief was the Crown-Prince Constantine).

Just after this new glorious period in the History of Hellenism, the Ist World War began. Greece continued to fight at the side of its Western allies, whereas Turkey had sided with the Central Powers (Germany and Bulgaria). El. Venizelos understood the great opportunity immediately. His allies repeatedly had told him: "Go ahead": And the Greek army victoriously advanced in eastern Thrace, in South Russia, in Asia Minor, where in May 1919 entered the port of Smyrna as a liberator. (One year later the Treaty of Sevres granted Greece Smyrna and its hinterland, August 1920). This decision must not surprise the reader as Asia Minor (ancient Ionia) had always been in the hands of the Greeks since at least the XIII c. B.C., with a compact Greek population which kept its national Hellenic conscience, religion, and all Greek customs. So this decision of the allies of Greece was based on the principle of "Nationalities". (In Asia Minor there were at that moment 2.118 Greek schools, and 2.139 Orthodox churches).

After Turkey's capitulation in October 1918, the Greek troops entered Constantinople together with the allies and Greek warships anchored in the Bosphorus. The thousands of Greeks who lived there under the Turks could not believe what their ears heard: it was the national Anthem of Greece from the Greek battleship "Averoff". A liturgy followed in the Church of St. Sophia. This moment was the

118

The Cretan Eleftherios Venizelos, Prime Minister of Greece (1910-1920) and (1928-1932), creator of great Greece. He died in Paris in 1936. His tomb is at his native city Chania, in Crete.

fulfilment of the fondest dreams of Hellenism!

The Commander-in-chief of the Allied armed - Forces Franchet d'Esperay wrote to Venizelos on 3 December 1918: "At this moment when the hostilities are over, I eagerly wish to tell you how much the precious help of Greece to the allied troops of the East has been and how efficient the cooperation of the Hellenic army was; this permited me to finish successfully the decisive operations that you know of".

The Secreatry of State of Great Britain Lord Balfour, in his speach in London's Town-Hall on 9 november 1918 said: "The man who made Greece a noble collaborator in the noble collaboration of the free peoples is Venizelos, and the marvelous way in which the Greek army fought during the last operations against Germany and her ally Bulgaria, will eternally remain a brilliant page of the Hellenic history".

Even Clémenceau, the "Father of the Victory", after the capitulation of Bulgaria, was writing to Venizelos on 2 October 1918: "I am happy that I have the opportunity to greet Greece reborn and reconstituted and her distinguished leaders, who were able to lead her to the destiny she was deserving. Our victory in the East marks the beginning of the predominance of Justice".

And the Commander-in-chief of the British Forces pointed out: "Without the help of the Hellenic army the victory would have been inaccessible!"

Greece had participated in the operations of the East with 10 divisions. The casualties were 843 dead, 3.790 wounded, 671 missing. The losses in the merchant marine were enormous. Greece lost 68% of her ships, whereas Great Britain lost 43% and France 33%. Greek pilots of the Air-Force bombed the Dardanelles and Constantinople (a Greek pilot destroyed five German crafts). The casualties in Air-Force were 15 dead.

The great modern poet of Greece Kostis Palamas (1859-1943) was writing then:

"The grandeur of the nations is not counted by the acre,
but by the burning of the heart and shed of blood."

(Translated by the author)

120

The famous Greek battleship "Averoff" enters the harbour of Constantinople, with the fleet of the European allies after Turkey's capitulation on 14 November 1918.

The Greek "Evzones" paraded with the other allied armies at the Arc de Triomphe in Paris (photo at Benaki Museum), and Venizelos signed the Treaty of Sèvres (August 1920) which granted Greece Smyrna and its hinderland, as well as Eastern Thrace, the Dodecanese, Northern Epirus and Cyprus. The Greek Army would occupy Constantinople with the Allied Forces. This was the "Greece of the two continents and the five seas".

Neverthless disaster was not late to come. The centuries - old illness of the Hellenic nation: political disputes and envy, as well as the ploting of Italy, which did not like to see a Great Greece in the Mediterranean, lead to catastrophy: Venizelos lost the elections in November 1920, the policy of Greece towards the Western allies changed and the Treaty of Sèvres was not ratified. King Constantine who was pro-German, because of Queen Sophia (sister of the Kaïzer) came back from the exile and continued the war against the Turkey of Kemal Atatürk in Asia Minor, where the Greek army had advanced almost as far as Ankara. But the Hellenic nation was now divided in the Venizelists and the Royalists and this division was ravaging the army at the front. This army that had been victorious for 10 successive years (1912-1922) finally started to retreat. The historians have defined that it was not a defeat of the arms, but a moral defeat, due also to a certain neglect on the part of the government and bad supplying. The communist propaganda in the army was also a bad factor. (It is known that the Turks were supplied with munitions by the Soviet Russia and the Western Allies in order to fight against the Greeks). It was also the betrayal of Prince Nicolas who, at the last moment, withdrew a regiment at a decisive battle.

In his book "The secret Files of the Triple Entente" S.P. Cosmin remarks a cynic statement which had been heard in the French Parliament during the ratification of the Treaty of Lausanne (July 1923), responsible for the uprooting of Hellenism from Asia Minor and eastern Thrace: President Herriot reminded the deputies that **"It was thanks to France that the Turks were still in Constantinople!** "The cynism of the former allies of Greece goes beyond human understanding, when we think of the European ships in the harbour of Smyrna, which did not accept on board the Greek refugees that swam out to them getting away from the flames of the burning Smyrna, and the Turkish slaughter at the water-front. The

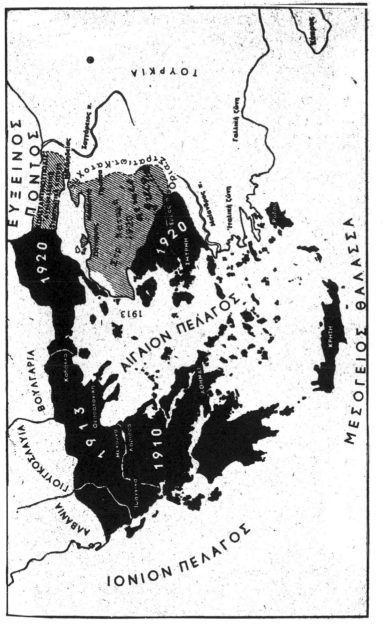

ΕΥΞΕΙΝΟΣ ΠΟΝΤΟΣ

ΤΟΥΡΚΙΑ

Οράς Στρατιωτ. Κατοχ.

1920

1920

1913

ΣΜΥΡΝΗ

ΑΙΓΑΙΟΝ ΠΕΛΑΓΟΣ

ΒΟΥΛΓΑΡΙΑ

Καβάλα

1913

Θεσσαλονίκη

ΓΙΟΥΓΚΟΣΛΑΥΙΑ

ΑΛΒΑΝΙΑ

Μπίτολα

Ιωάννινα

1910

ΑΘΗΝΑΙ

ΚΡΗΤΗ

ΜΕΣΟΓΕΙΟΣ ΘΑΛΑΣΣΑ

ΙΟΝΙΟΝ ΠΕΛΑΓΟΣ

The map of Greece in 1920, after the Treaty of Sèvres, which was a diplomatic success of Eleftherios Venizelos, based on the glorious victories of the Hellenic army, during the I World War.

123

A street of Constantinople (Stavrodromiou) decorated with Greek flags in 1918. In those days 400.000 Greeks were living in Constantinople under Turkish rule. Since the capitulation of Turkey the Hellenic army occupied this city with the western allies. (1918-1922). Photo: archives of "Luridis Foundation "Memories of Constantinople", 12, Vas. Sophias Ave. Athens 106.74, Tel. 7219-503.

Consul of the United-States in Smyrna George Horton said: "I am ashamed to belong to the human race". (September 1922). More than one million were the victims of the slautering in all Asia Minor and the Pontus (eastern part of the Black Sea), and one and a half million the refugees who came to Greece, possessing nothing but the clothes they were wearing. In the Benaki Museum one can see some precious ecclesiastical objects from the Orthodox Churches of Asia Minor, that the refugees managed to save. At New Procopion in the island of Eubea, a village of refugees from Procopion of Asia Minor, is to be seen the miraculous intact relic of St. John the Russian that the refugees transported from their fatherland. And behind the Metropolitan Church of Athens we can see the statue of the Bishop of Smyrna Chrysostom, who was lynched by the Turks (1922). Since then the Seven Churches of Asia (the Christian communities) mentioned in the Revelation do not exist any more. There are no Orthodox Christians in Asia Minor and all the cities and villages lost their Greek names and have Turkish names. (The excavations have proved their Hellenic character as well as the existance of Byzantine churches).

The Treaty of Lausanne (24 July 1923) which has been the coronation of the disaster "was established to the detriment of the European interests; it certainly abolished the most positive results of the victory of the Allies in the East" ("The Secret Files of the Triple Entente", S.P. Cosmin, Nouvelle Editions Latines, Paris 1969).

The Period of the Ist Republic (1924-1935)

The loss of Asia Minor has been concidered by the historians a more calamitous event, than the fall of Constantinople in 1453, because this time the uprooting was radical, because of the mass-slaughtering and the flight of the refugees. Only the Greek population of Constantinople (named since then Istanbul), was spared, as well as that of the two Greek islands at the entrance of the Dardanelles Imbros and Tenedos that the Western Allies granted to Turkey, in spite of the principle of the "Nationalities". This Greek minority in Turkey like all other minorities, according to the Treaty of Lausanne ought to be respected, but the Turks little by little transgressed this Treaty by forcing the Greeks to leave, because of

125

very hard measures against them. Of the 400.000 Greeks who were living in Constantinople till the Ist World War, hardly 3.000 remain today. Whereas the Turkish minority in Greece is growing continously! (in eastern Macedonia and in the islands of Rhodes and Cos in the Dodecanese).

Greece after the confusion of the catastrophe of Asia Minor, entered a period of political disputes, a period of great instability and of economic and social disorder. She also had to provide food, housing and work for 1.500.000 new citizens, the refugees, who were in complete misery (a unique case in the history of modern states). Neverthless this new Ionic element was an infusion of new blood to Greek life. The refugees from Asia Minor played a vital role in all the branches of society, in industry and business, in literature and fine Arts.

The Republic which was proclaimed on 25 March 1924 was very weak, in spite of the good intentions of its first leader Alex. Papanastassiou. Coups-d'Etat of the army succeeded one another and the propaganda of the communist party was reinforced by poverty. It was then that the Ministry of Agriculture and the Bank of Agriculture were founded, as well as the Bank of Greece.

Eleftherios Venizelos followed the political affairs of the country from abroad. Finally he came back to Greece and won the elections on 19 August 1928. His government which tried to solve many problems, even to inaugurate a friendship with the Turkey of Kemal, ended in 1932. A great political disorder and instability followed, and after a Coup-d'Etat of the Republicans without success (1935), Venizelos returned to Paris where he died in March 1936. The French newspapers wrote those days: "Every hundred years such a diplomatic genius appears in the world".

The political passions had attained such a crescendo, as to lead to the restoration of the Monarchy in 1935 (George II came back from exile after a plebiscite 97%), and to the dictator John Metaxas, ex-high officer of the Hellenic army (4 August 1936). So the prophetic words of the ancient Greek philosopher Aristotle were fulfiled once more in Greece: Tyranny (dictatorship) follows a corrupted Republic".

Within four years John Metaxas managed to reorganize the country depending only on domestic economic sources, without

The Ecumenical Patriarch Athinagoras I, among the ruins of destroyed Orthodox churches by the Turkish mob on 6-7 September 1955. Of the 83 old Byzantine churches with mosaics of great art, only 5 or 6 survive after this night of terror. Photo: Dem. Caloumenos.

The Commitee of the World Council of Churches verifies the vandalism of the Turks in a Greek cemetery of Constantinople in September 1955. Photo of the documentary book "The Crucifixion of Christianity", Athens 1978 by Dem. Caloumenos.

foreign loans. It was under his government that Social Insurance was founded for the first time in Greece. He also succeeded in reinforcing the morale of the people so much that when the sirens of the war sounded on 28 October 1940, the Greeks like one soul rushed to defend their fatherland.

Note: The final uprooting of the Greeks from Turkey took place, against the International Law, in September 1955, when the Turkish government of Menderes permitted a fanatic mob (helped even by the police), to destroy all the Greek shops and most of the Greek houses, all the churches and cemeteries in Constantinople and Smyrna, even the tombs of the Patriarchs, in order to express their discontent against the referendum of the Greek Cypriots (1950), who were demanding the respect of the Charter of the United Nations and the principle of "Self-Determination". This right had been granted to all the colonies except Cyprus, because of the economic interests of Britain in the Middle-East.

Great Britain had forgotten her promises to return Cyprus to Greece, during the II World War, when the young Greek-Cypriots were fighting at her side as volonteers. The Turks had possessed Cyprus in 1571 when this conquest was followed by a massacre of the entire population of Nicosia, and other atrocities. In 1878 they sold Cyprus to Britain, and although it is known that a sold thing cannot be reclaimed, Turkey stepped into the scene as a claimant, under the auspices of the British Government.

The Greeks who live now in Turkey; in Constantinople and in the islands Imbros and Tenedos, are Turkish subjects. No Greek subject has the right to live constantly in Turkey. Even the members of the Orthodox Ecumenical Patriarchate are Turkish subjects!

The Period of the II World War
The New Hellenic Epic (1940-1950)

"Liberty is a holy passion.
And once more in the twentieth century
she gave her battle
on this soil that has nourished us".

Angelos Terzakis, contemp. Greek writer
Translated by the author.

A short time before attacking Greece officially, Italy proved her treachery by a filthy crime:

On 15 August 1940 in Tinos, the island of the Holy Virgin, where there is treasured her miraculous icon, discovered in 1823 by vision to a nun, Greece was celebrating the great feast of the Dormi-

129

tion of the Holy Virgin, and the Greek State was represented by a warship, the cruiser "Helli". Its crew was to participate in the religious procession. At 8.30 a.m. however the "Helli" was torpidoed by an Italian sumbarine and sunk in the harbour. We can see today the fragments of the torpedoes which bear, engraved on the metal, the name of the Italian industry, in the Maritime Museum of Greece close to the harbour Zea in Piraeus.

Greece (a neutral country then) was officially attacked by Italy at her north-west border (Albania) on 28 October 1940 at 5.30 a.m. after an ultimatum which had been presented to the Prime Minister John Metaxas at 3 a.m. at home, by the Italian Embassador.

John Metaxas at this critical moment did not have the time to consult either the Ministers or the Greek people, but he had milleniums of Greek history before him and he gave his answer: "No, we shall not let you pass!" And since then the day of 28 October is called the "No-day", and every year the Greeks celebrate it as national holiday.

The attack took place before the expiration of the ultimatum and immediately the small Greek army, which defended the border, battled heroically for the fatherland. Italy, which, in those days was almost an empire had an army of 100.000 soldiers in Albania, while small Greece only 35.000. Italy was a country of 45.000.000 inhabitants and Greece of 7.000.000. Italy had an Air-Force of 400 aircrafts and Greece only 140 and not very good ones. The Italian navy in the Mediterranean was second after that of Great Britain; Greece had only 16 warships of slow speed and only 6 submarines. The front on the Albanian border was 240 km long, but on the Greek side it was very mountainous, almost inaccessible, and the transport of soldiers and supplies was very difficult, whereas on the side in Albania, there was a road which facilitated transportation.

In spite of the hard conditions under which the Hellenic army was fighting: steep mountains, snow tempests, bad supplying (soldiers often had nothing to eat but dry bread, and wear boots with wholes in their soles), the morale of the soldiers was very high. A British reporter who was at the front wrote: "The Greek soldiers live as saints and fight as heroes". The world was astonished to hear of the victories of small Greece, when European countries much more powerful and better equiped had surrendered very rapidly.

The procession of the miraculous icon of the Holy Virgin. During this celebration many miracles take place every year on 15 August on the island of Tinos. We can distinguish the sailors and officers of the Hellenic Navy.

The President of South Africa Jan Smuts said then: "Till now we used to say that the Greeks fight like heroes, henseforht we shall say that heroes fight like Greeks". (Manchester Guardian 19-4-41).

General De Gaule said: "The struggle of Greece and her achievements grant her unquestionable rights".

The Secretary of State of Great Britain Anthony Eden said: "If the Mediterranean schedule of Hitler, which failed thanks to the victorious resistance of Greece, had succeeded, the German attack against Russia would have had different results. The fighters of Pindus and the rest, together with the fighters at Marathon, will be the leaders and they will englighten in the future centuries the whole world".

The commander-in-chief of the Middle East Wavell said: "We acknowledge with pleasure that our Greek allies were the first who, with the glorious victories in Northern Epirus, opened the way to victory and gave a decisive blow against fascist Italy. This success was not oly of a local importance, but influenced the course of the war. The defense of Crete saved Cyprus, Syria, and Irac and may be Tobrouk" (harbour of Lybia).

Moscow broadcasted: "As Russians and as men we are grateful to you, because thanks to your sacrifices we gained the necessary time to prepare our defense. Greeks, we are grateful to you".

How can we explain this superhuman success? There is an explanation beyond logic; it was the Orthodox Christian faith which reinforced the soldiers. It was the Holy Virgin who many times appeared in vision at the front to give them courage, and who had been insulted by the Italians during Her Feast at Tinos. These battles of giants, which, as historians recognised, were unprecedent in history, had acquired a religious character. (An eye-witness asserted that he and the whole regiment of the "Evzones of Central Greece" saw in vision St. George on his horse ahead of them opening the way, at the beginning of the first attack of the Hellenic army. When the regiment saw this vision felt such an enthousiasm that shouted the famous war cry of the Greeks: "aera" (air) and started to run ahead. St. George is the patron-saint of the Hellenic infantry. When this fighter of 1940 was relating this event 20 years later he was shivering as if he could still see St. George in front of him).

The Greek soldiers were also drunk with history. All the past

The Greek soldiers, as real eagles, advance on the snow-covered mountains of Northern Epirus liberating the Greek populations and pushing backwards the Italian army of Mussolini, so powerful in those days. These soldiers with very simple means, by their successive victories gave courage to the countries of Europe that had already surrendered. (Painting of the Greek artist Alex. Alexandrakis, 1913-1968, who fought at the first line and made the sketches on the spot).

centuries and their glorious ancestors were fighting in them. This fact has been very well expressed by the great poet of contemporary Greece, Costis Palamas still living at that time:

"I don't have other words to say.
I have only this one;
Make yourselves drunk with the wine
of "Eighteen and twenty one".

Translated by the author

The great success of the Greek troops to thwart the Italian attack in spring 1941 (9-15 March), that Moussolini had thoroughly prepared, has been considered the end of the war for Italy. This is why Hitler decided to attack Greece in his turn.

The German attack took place at the Bulgarian border (north eastern Greece) against the "Metaxa line": superb fortification work for those days, that John Metaxas had prepared hastily during the four years of his government with what little financial means Greece could afford then. So on 6th April 1941 Greece had to struggle against two enemies at the same time at two different fronts: one in Northern Epirus, where the Greek army had advanced victorious, and the other one at the Bulgarian border. This time it was too much for Greece and in spite of a heroic resistance of four days the Germans entered the Greek territory by the Yougoslavian border, which was not guarded, because of an alliance treaty between Greece and Yougoslavia. After Yougoslavia's capitulation the passage was free for the German troops, who took the Greek soldiers in the rear. The German officers were amazed to see the small number of the defenders of the country, and out of admiration they offered military honours to the Greek soldiers. So Greece had the right to her flag during the German occupation, because the flag had not been dishonoured. On the Acropolis of Athens two flags were waving, the Greek and the German. The Greek officers had also the right to their uniform and sword.

The Germans advancing southwards met with the resistance of the Greek troops and the British expedition (Australians and New Zealanders) sent at the last moment. The last battle in Greece took place in Crete in May 1941, where all the population of the island struggled against the German parachutists, the elite corps of the Ger-

134

This is how Greece was fighting in 1940-41. Detail from a painting by Alex. Alexandrakis. Dragonas Coll.

man army, which was almost completely destroyed. The heroic resistance of the Cretans, of the Greek army and of the British expedition averted the danger of a similar attack by air against the Middle-East and Malta, because after the battle of Crete Hitler never used parachutists again.

After the fall of Crete (due mostly to a bad wireless communication) the Greek government with the King (who was till the last moment in Crete), left for Egypt and so did a part of the Greek army and the rest of the navy, in order to continue the struggle with the Western allies beyond their country, in northern Africa. Their heroism was great even away from Greece at the famous battle of the desert at el-Alamein (50 km to west of Alexandria) in 1942, and at the battle of Rimini in Italy in September 1944. The liberation of Greece started from the south as the Germans were slowly withrawing towards the north. The liberation of Athens took place on 12 October 1944.

During all this supreme effort of Greece for liberty, which was the starting point of the final victory for the allies (a historical fact recognised by the diplomatic, military and political personalities of that time), **Turkey was completely neutral!** So is it not an injustice towards history that Turkey is today possessing the Presidency of the Council of Europe?

Here is a statement of a political personality during the II World War about Greece: Anthony Eden Secretary of State of Great Britain was saying in those days:"

"Greece was the first to give Moussolini an unforgetable lesson. It was she who caused the national revolution against the Axis in Yugoslavia, it was she who delayed the Germans on her continental territory and in Crete for six weeks, it was she who overturned the chronological order of all the schedules of the German General Staff, and it was she who brought a radical change to the evolution of its expeditions and perhaps to the issue of the war."

This small Greece whom, in those days, everybody was praising and whom, later on, her allies betrayed (especially in the case of Cyprus), in order to defend her liberty and the liberty of free Europe, only during the war against the Italians (28.10.1940 - 6.4.1941) had suffered:

136

The map of Northern Epirus in 1913, when it was liberated by the Hellenic army during the Balkan Wars, and when all the Greek churches and schools were still functioning. This is the area of the new Epic of the Hellenic army (second liberation) in 1940-41. This purely Greek province, twice liberated by victorious battles was not annexed to Greece because of the negative policy of her European allies. Photo of the "History of contemporary Greece", by Sp. Markezinis vol. 1920-22. Publ. Papyros, Athens, 1973.

```
13.308 killed and 42.485 wounded in the army
  201    »                    in the navy
   67    »                    in the Air-Force
```

Even Hitler in his speech at the Reichstag on 5th May 1941 acknowledged: "Among all our adversaries who have confronted us, only the Greek soldier has battled with a great valour and a supreme disdain towards death." During these battles (6-9 April 1941) the Germans did not make a prisoner of any Greek soldier.

Neverthless the sacrifices in human lives were much greater among the people of the country. The number of dead civilians is 500.000 which constituted in that time 12% of the whole Greek population. The road and train network was completely destroyed and the merchant marine lost 73% of its capacity, moreover 1.700 villages were completly destroyed. Greece was like an immense cemetery.

But the Greek soul resisted admirably. When the Germans threatened the Archbishop of Athens Damaskinos to shoot him, he answered: "In this country the enemies usually do not shoot the bishops, they hung them".

The triple occupation (German, Italian and Bulgarian) caused 68.000 executions, 190.000 prisoners and 88.000 deported.

The casualties of Greece during the battles in the desert of northern Africa are:

```
  344 killed and 606 wounded in the army
  309    »                    in the navy
   89    »                    in the Air-Force
```

The sacrifices of Greece during the II World War went beyond her possibilities: 41% of the national income was lost, an income that was not even sufficient at the begining of the war.

The government which was formed after the liberation (23.10.1944) under George Papandreou had scheduled the reconstruction of the country. But suddenly a new factor appeared: the betrayal of the blood-stained fatherland. The legal government of 23 October (in which six communist Ministers participated) required the disarmament of the partisans, as the German occupation was over. But, contrarily to what had happened in the western countries of Europe on that occasion, the Greek communist Ministers refused

Greek soldiers receive the holy blessing by a priest before setting on for a patrol in the desert of Lybia. (II World War). Photo from the "Exhibition of the Military History of the Hellenes", vol. II, 1968.

The "Famine in 1941" in Greece by Alex. Alexandrakis. The artist's coll.
Photo of the "Exhibition of the Military History of the Hellenes" vol. II,
1968.

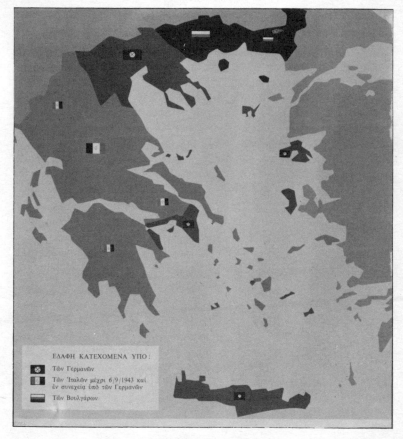

ΕΔΑΦΗ ΚΑΤΕΧΟΜΕΝΑ ΥΠΟ:

Τῶν Γερμανῶν

Τῶν Ἰταλῶν μέχρι 6/9/1943 καὶ
ἐν συνεχείᾳ ὑπὸ τῶν Γερμανῶν

Τῶν Βουλγάρων

*The occupation in Greece, by the Germans, the Italians and the Bulgarians.
To the latter the Germans had offered eastern Macedonia and western
Thrace in return for the free passage through their country to the German
army when they attacked Greece.*

to obey. They all resigned (1.12.1944) and the great demonstration of the communists in Athens on 3.12.1944, although prohibited, marked the beginning of the barricade war in all the area of the capital, in order to impose an illegal communist power of a small minority by force. Their crimes during December 1944 in the area of Athens were awful: more than 65.000 Greeks (men and women) were slaughtered among them:

     275 priests
     239 teachers
     120 physicians
     264 syndicalists (trade-union leaders)
and 48.000 deported

The defeat of these criminals (crimes of Common Law) by a small number of Greek defenders saved Western Europe: a new "Salamis" took place at the crossroads south-west of the Acropolis in December 1944.

At this point of the city, during the first week of December, 400 brave men of the Athenian gendarmery plus 20 officers of the army sropped the passage of 5.000 armed communists, who wanted to reach the centre where the government was. Thousands of others were arriving from different parts of the country. The communist troops in the mountains (the partisans) instead of continuing their resistance against the retreating Germans and hinder their escape, they were letting them go without stopping them, and they rapidly descended towards Athens in order to take power in an illegal way. Even Churchill visited Athens after this decisive battle, in order to have full comprehension of the events, and the report of the British Whig deputy Walter Citrine is an objective document on the slaughterings of civilians (10.000).

Note: The historical building of the Athenian Gendarmery dates from King Otho's reign (XIX c.), it has been restored and became the museum of the Acropolis history.

After these sad events the Prime Minister George Papandreou resigned, the Archbishop of Athens Damaskinos was named regent, (as the King was abroad), and the new government of Nicolas Plastiras (General of the Hellenic army, who had saved what could be saved of the army in Asia Minor in 1922), signed the famous

"Agreement of Varkiza" (south suburb of Athens), on 12 February 1945, which granted amnesty, in order to establish normal life. Neverthless the communists did not appreciate the pardon of their native land. In January 1946 they began again to attack the people in different parts of the country, but especially on the eve of the elections of March 1946 (in which they refused to participate), they started a new revolt at Litochoron, a village at the foot of Mt. Olympus by attacking the police-station, thus inaugurating a new period of blood-shed.

They started this new revolt after having been organized and trained in the military schools of the communist Balkan countries (Albania, Yugoslavia and Bulgaria), from where they received also their arms. The northern border of Greece of 1.000 km was not guarded, as the national army had come as liberator from the south. So the passage through the border was very easy after the end of the war.

This fratricidal war which was actually instigated by these three enemies of Greece lasted till August 1949. It was an extremely difficult and bloody war, because the communist guerrillas also attacked the villages, burnt them, committed crimes and forced enrolment. The great difficulty was due to the fact that there was no regular front. It was a guerrilla war.

One of the most horrible acts was the kidnapping of thousands of Greek children, even of babies not yet baptised, by the communists, who took them to the countries of the "iron curtain" where they turned them into enemies of their country by a special education, as the Turks had done in the Middle Ages. (The documents of this event are in the archives of the International Red Cross in Geneva, based on the applications of the parents, where the age of the children is mentioned).

The proof that this fratricidal war was instigated by the Balkan satelites of Russia, is based on the report of the United Nations Commitee, which visited the northern border of Greece for an objective investigation at the beginning of 1947.

After this report, on 12 March 1947, the President of the United-States Harry Truman delivered a famous speech at the Congress in which he explained why financial aid to Greece was essential at this difficult moment. The following excerpt of his speech is engraved on a marble slab in English and in Greek close to his statue that the Greek-Americans, thankfully, erected in Athens (King Constantine Ave. Hilton area).

"I believe that it must be the policy of the United-States to support free peoples who are resisting attempted subjugation. If Greece should fall under the control of an armed minority, confusion and disorder might well spread throughout the entire Middle-East. Moreover the disappearance of Greece as an independent state, would have a profound effect upon those countries in Europe, where peoples are struggling against great difficulties to maintain their freedoms and their independence, while they repair the damages of war. Should we fail to aid Greece in this fateful hour, the effect will be far reaching to the West and to the East. We must take immediate and resolute action".

Since beginning of the year 1949 the tactics of the Hellenic army changed because of the strategic genius of Marshal Alex. Papagos (who had also been Commander-in-chief, during the war against the Italians in Northern Epirus in 1940-41). So he was recalled at this extremely dangerous moment as the leader of the national Greek army.

The strategic genius of Marshal Papagos, the financial aid of the United-States, the heroism of the national army and the detachment of Yugoslavia from the Sovietic Block (28.6.1948), when she stopped permitting the passage through her border to the communist Greek guerrillas, were the factors which saved Greece from the "iron curtain" and helped her to become the "southern shield" of free Europe.

The cost of this new effort for liberty (1946-1949) was immense:

- 120.000 dead (civilians and millitary)
- 28.000 children deported to the "iron curtain"
- 3.050 military prisoners deported to the "iron curtain"
- 20.000 civilians prisoners deported to the "iron curtain"
- 750.000 refugies homeless because of the destruction of villages and of the dangers of the war.
- 100.000 left the country willingly for the countries of the "iron curtain".

The material cost was estimated to $ 900.000.000.

144

Marshal Alex. Papagos, Commander - in - Chief of the Hellenic army during the II World War, and also in the years of the communist threat. His tactics secured the victory of Greece over the danger of the Communist totalitarianism in Europe.

One of the goals of the Communist party was the detachement of Macedonia from Greece and its attachment to the Slav world, according to a decision of the International Communist Party in 1924. This goal has been the century-old desire of the Slavs since the Byzantine period, when the Byzantin Emperors had very often to undertake wars against these peoples which had been ennoying the Empire, since their installation in the Balkan peninsula (600-800 A.D.).

Note: All the historical information of this chapter is based on the "Exhibition of the Military History of the Hellenes", vol. II 1968, Ed. of the Hellenic army, and on "Modern Greek History", by Prof. A. Vacalopoulos, Salonica, 1979.

If Greece had not won the battle of Athens (December 1944) and the war in the mountains (1946-1949), the history of Western Europe would have been different today. Greece was the shield which saved the free world during the I and the II World Wars. (This fact has been acknowledged by personalitites of those days, as it has been already mentioned).

And as if so many sacrifices were not sufficient, Greece, also participated in the Corean War together with the other country-members of the United Nations in 1950 by sending 1.000 soldiers and 9 air-crafts, of which four were lost. By this participation Greece was conforming to the Charter of the United Nations (articles 43-44). This Greek batallion took part in many decisive battles and the Greek airmen made 13.777 hours of flight. The Greek flag was decorated by the Commander-in-Chief of the allied Forces in Corea.

After the war of Corea Greece has enjoyed peace, except for the problem of Cyprus and the illegal revendications of Turkey in the Aegean Sea which is Greek territory according to the International Law. The behaviour of Turkey has obliged Greece to live constantly in a state of alert, and to spend important sums of money on national defense.

Greece after 1950

"After 1950 the Greeks resumed the effort for the reconstruction of the Economy, but they went beyond a simple answer to material need. They surpassed "measure". They forgot the moderation and frugality, which has always characterised the national life,

146

"Helen" a painting of the leading Greek artist and professor at the School of Fine Arts in Athens, Andrew Georgiades" the Cretan", (1892-1981).

and strove after affluence. Money and luxury became an end in itself.

This was the consequence of a policy, which had rased the flag of the "Capital" as a standard to such an extent that even the workers' classes were affected. There is of course a prosperity, but it is one of bad quality, because the spiritual side was neglected.

The political leaders forgot that Greece achieved greatness in the past centuries only when she was guided by the spiritual elevation which faith in Christ grands, as the case was with the war of 1940-41.

Neverthless it is possible to bring the culturer treasures out of the silence of the museums and the libraries and nourish with them the soul of the people once again. So the nation enriched and enlivened with its heritage will give birth to a "Third civilisation", the "Modern Greek civilisation".

The means for the fulfilment of this object are: frugality which gives dignity and self-sufficiency and grants inner freedom and possibility of spritual fructification; collaboration between leaders and people in the spirit of the Apostolic faith and Christian love; unity in order to reach the ultimate goal: the creation of a civilisation which will bear the fruits of the living Christian Apostolic faith to all humanity in free will and peace. "(The free will of those who accept the Christian faith is mentioned in Matt. 16, 24 and Rev. 3,20).

Extract from the book "Kindling" by Lucy Metaxa.
Transl. by the author.

Undoubtedly the builders of this civilisation will be true members of the Orthodox Church (the Mother-Church), because mystic life is indispensable for those who want to participate in the cunstruction of Christ's Church. Mistic life evolves participation in the liturgical life and the Holy Sacrements (Confession - Communion) as it has been handed down to us by the Apostles and defended by the Seven Ecumenical Councils. Life in Christ will make possible the enlightment of the Holy-Spirit and the observance of the will of God in our personal life, and this will lead to the gradual sanctification of the whole humanity. (John 10, 16) (Matt. 13, 33) (Rev. 20, 1-6) (Daniel 2,35).

The centuries smile from the metopes of Phidias.
The centuries smile from the church of St. Sophia,
on the modest jugs of the Turkish-yoke days,
and in the song "Myrtia" of our days."

Poem of the author
24 February 1988

Folk costume of Attica (area of Athens), drawing of Athena Tarsouli. It expresses the elegance and nobility of the Greek woman before the western influence of European fashion.

The biblical outline of the modern Greek civilisation on the way of its shaping

The Biblical outline in which the plan of God for the salvation of mankind and his final glorification is evolving - an eternal world plan - which is unfolding its images in a marvelous way on the frescoes and mosaics of the Byzantine and Post-Byzantine churches during almost 2.000 years is the following:

Old Testament:

a) The creation of the universe and of man by the Trinitarian God (Genesis 1, 1-31) (2, 1-25) (John 1,1). The Trinitarian God in the Genesis is expressed by the word "Elohim", (the word for "God" **in the plural,** in old Hebrew in Gen. 1,1 as well as in many other passages).

b) The fall of man (because of the bad use of his freedom) and education (in freedom) of humanity by God (Law, Prophets, the "spermatic Word" for the pagans).

New Testament:

c) The Incarnation of God (the second Person of the Holy Trinity), who became man in the person of Jesus Christ, in order to deïfy man (John I).

d) The Crucifixion: the passion, the suffering of God-Man (only in his human nature) in order to be victorious upon sin and death by His complete obedience to God the Father, obedience which made Him the "second Adam" (a heroic Adam and not a fallen one), able now to give the possibility of salvation to those who would accept it in freedom.

e) The Resurrection: the proof of His divinity and His continuous union with His Father, who raised Him from the dead. His victory on death gave Him the possibility to enter Hell victorious and liberate from the chains of death those who had lived on the Earth before Him (I. Pet. 3,19).

f) The Ascension to Heaven in the presence of the Angels: (the Angels were present also at the Incarnation (Luk. 1,26 - Luk. 2,9), at the Passion (Luk. 22,43) and at the Resurrection (Luk. 24,4). a fact which proves his last words to His disciples before leaving the Earth:

"All power is given unto me in heaven and in earth. Go ye therfore, and teach all nations, baptizing them in the name of the Father and the Son and of the Holy Ghost: teaching them to observe all things whatsoever I have commanded you: and lo, I am with you alway, even unto the end of the world." (Matt. 28, 18-20).

The Ascension also proves the fulfilment of the promise for the sending of the Holy Spirit to the Apostles, which will make of them the first bishops (all equal in Grace). He had said to them: "It is expedient for you that I go away: for if I go not away, the Comforter will not come unto you; but if I depart, I will send Him unto you" (John 16,7). He had said too: "I will not leave you orphans: I will come to you. Yet a little while, and the world seeth me no more; but ye see me: because I live, ye shall live also. (John 14, 18-19).

g) The Pentecost: The descent of the Holy Spirit to the Apostles ten days after the Ascension is the fulfilment on His promise of this sending and the beginning of the activity of the Church in the world and its historical expansion, which continues till the present day (in spite of the persecutions), and which will continue till the final accomplishment (in freedom), till the final glorification of man and the universe: the Eternal Kingdom of God (I. Cor. 15 and Rev. 21).

All this plan is not metaphysics, but history. Outside this historical cycle the world lives in disintegration and eternal death. The persons, the societies and the nations who would advance in a free way towards this path of the "Transfiguration", which constitutes the real salvation, they should change little by little their being of "fallen man" into the being of "Grace" by their participation in the Holy Eucharist (of the Apostolic and Universal Church: the Orthodox Church), where the created man in communion with the "non-created" (the "non-created energies" of the Holy Trinity), reaches Eternity and is deïfed.

The means for this gradual change are those that the Apostolic Church grants to her children: prayer (especially the short "prayer of the heart": "Jesus Christ, Son of God, our Lord, have mercy upon me", or "upon us", repeated mentally in any time and in any place), asceticism: (obedience to the will of God in the personal life), participation in the Holy Sacraments (confession and Holy Communion), the various religious services and the Feasts of the great events of Salvation.

So the Christian faith according to the Holy Bible, practiced in all its purity and plenitude (the Orthodox Church) includes:

— "The truth for God, for the world and for man.

— The Holy Bible (in its whole) and the Holy Apostolic Traditions (written and oral: II. Thess. 2,15).

— The struggle (spiritual, not by force) for the growth and the construction of the Church (Kingdom of God on the Earth as presented in a very interesting way by one of the most ancient Fathers of the Church, Hermas, II c. A.D., in his book "the Shepherd" (Vision III ch. I-VII in Migne P.G.).

— The dogmatic decisions and the canons of the Seven Ecumenical Councils. (Ist. Ecum. Council in 325 A.D. and the last in 787 A.D.).

— The perfect union of the dogmatic truth with the personal life of the believers.

— The blood and the relics of the Saints (because they transmit Grace).

— The cult of the holy icons. (Symbolic presence of the "Church in Triumph" in Heaven and symbolic expression of the incarnation of God).

— The asceticism of the monks and the nuns in the monasteries and of the people of God in the world. (The monastic life is biblical: (I. Kings, 19) (Matt. 3,1 and 4,1-4) (Marc 1, 4-5) (Luk. 3 and 4) (John 1, 23) (Matt. 19, 12).

— The Works of charity, as well as the effort for justice that the believers individually and the Church in an organized way fulfil in the world.

The strife of every believer to meet Jesus, a strife which continues till death, and his participation in the "Kingdom prepared since the foundation of the world" (Matt. 25, 34).

All this accepted in a free way in full conscience, practiced in a constant struggle which will end with life (may-be by martyrdom according to the Revelation: "Be thou faithful unto death and I will give thee the crown of life". (Rev. 2,10) constitutes Orthodoxy".

Extract from the essay: "Militant
Orthodoxy" by Rev. Const. Fouskas
"Koenonia" Sept. 1987, transl. by the author.

This treasure which is at the disposal of all those who would like to acquire it, Greece, which is the only free Orthodox country in the world (the other Orthodox countries live under the pressure of atheist totalitarianism), is able to communicate in freedom, as teaching and as experience of life, in order to fulfil the real unity of Europe and later on of the whole world. Because this Apostolic teaching and this experience of life are able to lead little by little the societies to advance and to maximize the human efficiency in all fields, even in politics.

Since in our days we display such a zeal for the improvement of agricultural or industrial products, why should we not endeavour for the improvement of man, who is the agent of civilisation?

As we graft the tree in order to get better fruits, why should we not graft man on the Victor of Death, who is also the source of all goodness, in order to create the real civilisation, the civilisation which will not only be interested in the material side, but also in the moral one, since man has a dual nature (body and eternal soul-spirit)? Thus he will be able to acquire harmony and beatitude. In this way we will stop this spiritual starvation which reigns at the present day in the societies of the western countries called "Christian", without mentioning the rest of humanity. In our days people are presenting the material starvation of the "Third World", without being anxious at all about the spiritual starvation of those who possess more than they need.

In the Psaulter we find the explanation of what we must do, so that we may not lack of the necessary:

"O taste and see that the Lord is good:
blessed is the man that trusteth in Him.
O fear the Lord, ye his saints:
for there is no want to them that fear Him.
Wealthy people lacked, and suffered hunger:
but they that seek the Lord
shall not want any good thing."

(Ps. 34, 8-10) King. James vers.

In this way man by his willing collaboration with God, as a conscious member of the Apostolic Church (the Orthodox Church) will be able to exercise his sacerdotal, prophetic and royal deaconship — the three gifts of the Lord that the Orthodox Christian is receiving at baptism and which become active after his conscious devotion to the Mother-Church.

Nowadays this plan is a living reality in Greece in places where the Holy Tradition is still part of everyday life, as well as in the Orthodox monastic communities, the best example of which is the pure Byzantine tradition of "Mt. Athos". Even in the big cities of Greece there are many families who still live this Christian Orthodox tradition in the everyday life, in spite of strong foreign influences.

The destiny of humanity is focused on the path that Christ followed towards the Calvery and the Resurrection, so that some day in the future the prophecy of Isaïah will be fulfiled:

"Thus saith God the Lord, he that created the heavens and streched them out; he that spread forth the earth, and that which cometh out of it; he that giveth breath unto the people upon it, and spirit to them that walk therein: I the Lord have called thee in righteousness, and will hold thine hand, and will keep thee, and give thee for a covenant of the people, for the light of the Gentiles; to open the blind eyes, to bring out the prisoners from the prison, and them that sit in darkness out of the prison house. I am the Lord: that is my name: and my glory will I not give to another, neither my praise to graven images. Behold, the former things are come to pass, and new things do I declare: before they spring forth I tell you of them.

Sing unto the Lord a new song, and his praise from the end of the earth, ye that go down to the sea, and all that is therein; the isles and the inhabitants thereof. Let the wilderness and the cities thereof lift up their voice, the villages that Kedar doth inhabit: let the inhabitants of the rock sing, let them shout from the top of the mountains. Let them give glory unto the Lord and declare his praise in the islands. The Lord shall go forth as a mighty man, he shall stir up jealously like a man of war: he shall cry, yea, roar; he shall prevail against his enemies.

I have long time holden my peace; I have been still, and refrained myself: now will I cry like a travailing woman; I will destroy and devour at once; I will make waste mountains and hills, and dry up all their herbs; and I will make the rivers islands, and I will dry up the pools. And I will bring the blind by a way that they knew not; I will lead them in paths that they have not known: I will make darkness light before them, and crooked thing straight. These things will I do unto them, and not forsake them. (Is. 42, 5-16).

EPILOGUE

As this book is addressed to the Western visitors of Greece it should be useful to refer to a literary master-piece of Europe: "The II. Faust" of Goethe, a drama which takes place in Medieval Sparta, in the Palace of Mystra, where Faust, who symbolizes the nordic Romanticism, meets Helen who symbolizes the classical spirit. From this union a boy is born: Euphorion, who is going to sacrifice himself for the supreme ideal which will lead him to Heaven.

In this drama, that Goethe wrote towards the end of his life, the reader is aware of the poet's change; in the "I. Faust" he is cultivating all the selfish passions at the point of selling his soul. In the "II. Faust", on the contrary, the poet is following clearly the path of repentance, mentionning even St. Mary of Egypt (who distinguished herself by an extreme repentance). Finally the hymn of the choir in the end of the play is praising the Virginal Motherhood whose Grace is imploring.

Neverthless the human being by excellence is the Holy Virgin (as she is presented to us in the Gospel and not as She appears in Roman Catholicism). The All Holy Mother of God, is the one who is constantly praying for our repentance in Heaven.

So it is not without any reason that this great poet ends his last work with this hope. It is not either without reason that this book, written in Greece, ends by an address to Her, who is the Patron of Christian Greece since the inauguration of Constantinople (330 A.D.), in order to beg Her constant intercession to the Holy Trinity, so that the Truth may shine all over and lead us to the final liberation:

"If ye continue in my word, then are ye my disciples indeed; and ye shall know the truth, and the truth shal make you free. (John 8, 31-32).

157

The Holy Virgin. A detail from the mosaic composition "The supplication", XIV c. A.D., in the women's gallery of st. Sophia in Constantinople. One of the greatest works of the Byzantine art.

Byzantine Hymn that the Orthodox Church uses
on 14 September, day of the first elevation and veneration of the
Cross,
after its discovery in Jerusalem by St. Helena
in 327 A.D.

"Cross, the protector of the whole universe.
Cross, the beauty of the Church.
Cross, the power of the Kings.
Cross, the support of the faithful.
Cross, the glory of the Angels
and wound of the demons".

Translated by the author

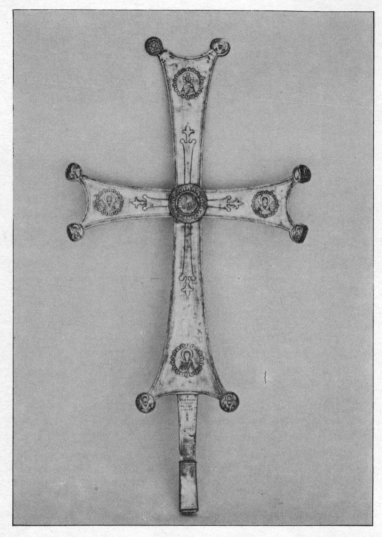

Byzantine Cross in silver from the Greek city of Adrianople (Eastern Thrace), X c. A.D., Athens, Benaki Museum.

MUSEUMS OF GREECE MENTIONED IN THE TEXT

Tel.

- Athens National Archeological Museum, 44 Patission st.   821.7724
- Archeological Museum of the Acropolis   323.6665
- Archeological Museum of the Agora (Attalos Portico)   321-0185
- Kerameikos Museum (ancient cemetery) 148, Hermou st.   346.3552
- Archeolog. Museum of Marathon, (by the tomb of the Plataeans)
- Byzantine Museum of Athens, 22, Ave. Vass. Sophias   721.1027
- Benaki Museum I, Koumbari st. Vass. Sophias Ave.   361.1617
- Soutzos Museum (Art National Galery) 50 Vas. Constandinou Ave.   721.1010
- War Museum (History of Greece), 2, Rizari st. (Vas. Sophias Ave).   721.5035
- National Historical Museum (Kolokotroni sq. Stadiou st.)   323.7617
- Eleftherios Venizelos Museum (1910-1920), 68, Vas. Sophias Ave.   775.0520
- "Goulandri Museum (Cycladic Art) 4, Neophytou Douka st.   723.4931
- "Goulandri" Museum (Natural History), 13, Levidou st. Kyfissia.   808.6405
- Folk Museum, 17, Kydathynaion st. (Placa)   321-3018
- Museum of Folk Tradition, 6 Ang. Hatzimichali st. (Placa)   324.3987
- Museum of the City of Athens (King Otho's period) Klafthmonos sq. (Stadiou st.)   324.6164
- Maritime Museum, Harbour of Zea in Piraeus.   451.6264
- Paleontoligical Museum (Univercity - City of Athens Kaissariani   724.7401

161

Peloponnese

- Archeolog. Museum of Argos (by the central sq.)
- Archeolog. Museum of Epidaurus (by the excavations)
- Archeolog. Museum of Nauplia (Constitution sq.).
- Folk Museum of Nauplia (by the harbour)
- Archeolog. Museum of Tripolis (in Arcadia), behind the church of the first sq.
- Archeolog. Museum of Lycossoura (in Arcadia, 15 km. from Megalopolis
- Archeolog. Museum of Olympia (by the excavations).
- Archeolog. Museum of Isthmia (by the Corinth Canal).
- Archeolog. Museum of Corinth (by the excavations of ancient Corinth).

Central Greece

- Archeological Museum of Thebes
- Archeological Museum of Delphi
- Archeological Museum of Volos
- House painted by the pop. painter Theophilos (Village Anakasia, House Kondou), suburb of Volos, at the foot of Mt. Pelion. (The villages of this mountain are dating from the XVIII c.: Macrinitsa, Portaria, Zagora etc.). — Miliès folk Museum.
- Museum of Larissa (Mosque).
- Traditional houses with frescoes at Ambelakia, Mt. Ossa 37 km to the North of Larissa (XVIII c.).
- Meteora Monasteries: XVIc. frescoes.
- Nicopolis Museum, by Preveza (western continental Greece).

Macedonia

- Archeolog. Museum of Salonica (by the International Fair).
- Folk Museum of Macedonia, 68, Vass, Olgas st. Salonica.
- Archeolog. Museum of Dion (by the town of Katerini, to the South of Salonica).
- Anthropolog. Museum of Petralona in Chalcidice (56 km from Salonica).

162

— Archeolog. Museum of Thassos (Ferry - boat from Keramoti to the East of Kavala).

Cyclades

— Archeolog. Museum of Delos
— Archeolog. Museum of Santorini (Phira).
— Archeolog. Museum of Myconos.
— Folk Museum of Myconos.
— Aegean Museum of Myconos.
— Museum of sculpture of Yannoulis Chalepas, island of Tinos (Pyrgos).

Crete

— Archeolog. Museum of Heraclion
— Historical Museum of Heraclion (Kalokairinou st.).
— Icons' Museum of Heraclion (by the church of St. Minas).

— Paleontol. Museum of Samos (Mitilinioi village).
— Museum of Theophilos (pop. painter, 3,5 km from Mitilini (Lesbos).

Dodecanese

— Archeolog. Museum of Rhodes (old city).
— Folk Museum of Rhodes (Symi sq.).
— Archeolog. Museum of the island of Kos (central sq.).

Islands of the Ionian Sea

— Byzantine Museum of Zakynthos.
— Museum of the National poet Dion. Solomos, 46, St. Marc sq. Zakynthos.
— Museum of the National poet Dion. Solomos, at the island of Corfu - Arseniou st. - Mourayia.

Touristic information about Cyprus in Athens, 36, Voucourestiou st., Ist. floor. Tel. 3610.178.

The house of the Greek National Poet Solomos in Corfu. (The light coloured house, which is today public library and museum.

APPENDIX
ABOUT MODERN GREEK CULTURE

"O divine, blood-covered fatherland!
How good are your black roks, and your
dry grass!"

Dion. Solomos
"The Cretan" (v. 40-42)

INFORMATION ABOUT THE MODERN GREEK CULTURE

In spite of the fact the Independent Greece has a rather short life (about 160 years), and that during this brief space of time the country was rarely in peace, the modern Greek culture is rather reach.

Painting was powerfully developed (even since the XVIII c. in the Ionian islands-western Greece), without forgetting the moving post-Byzantine frescoes in small chapels and monasteries all over Greece during the period of the Turkish domination (XV-XVIII c.).

The XIX c. sculpture of Greece is impressive (mostly neoclassical) and the XX c. one althought influenced by the western artistic current, shows now and then the orginality of the Greek spirit. Some Greek composers of classical music have already a place in the international repertories.

The visitor who would like to see works of Modern Greek painters and sculptors, may visit the National Art Gallery of painting and sculpture (Soutzos Museum) close to the Hilton of Athens.

Those who like contemporary classical music may find records of Greek composers of the XX c. at the record shops at the centre of Athens (Constitution sq. 3, Karageorgi Servias st.) as well as at the Union of Greek composers 38, Mitropoleos st., where they can also get records and scores of Greek composers free (Tel. 3223-302). We can also find scores of contemporary Greek composers at Nakas shop, 44, Panepistimiou st. (portico), Tel. 3612-720. The most complete collection of records and cassets of contemporary Greek classical music is at the shop "Neodisc", 25, Panepistimiou st. (Portico).

During this last period of peace (after 1950) Greece obtained twice the "Nobel Price" for poetry: George Seferis (1963) and Odysseus Elytis (1979).

The Greek handicraft so rich and so fine (not bad copies) is so

166

appreciated abroad, that the value of exportation attained 500.000 $ per year. (Information about work-shops and products: Headquarters of the National Handicraft Organisation, 9, Mitropoleos st. — Constitution sq. Tel. 3220-448). Shops of authentic copies: 6, Hypatias st. - behind the Metropolitan church of Athens, and 24, Voucourestiou st. by Constitution sq., as well as at the International Handicraft Organisation (UNESCO) — Hellenic department 17, Vryssakiou st. (behind Attalos Portico - Ancient Agora of Athens). A very interesting shop for Greek handicraft is at 59, Mitropoleos st. "Centre of Greek Tradition", (close to the Metrpolitan Church) Tel. 3213-023.

Some of the most famous painters of modern Greece at the Art National Gallery

- Nicephorus Lytras .... (1832-1904)
- Nicolas Chizis .... (1842-1901)
- George Iakovidis .... (1813-1932)
- Theodore Vryzakis .... (1814-1878)
- Theophilos (Pop. painter) .... (1873-1934)
- Const. Maleas .... (1879-1928)
- Sophia Lascaridou .... (1878-1965)
- Const. Parthenis .... (1878-1967)
- Photis Kondoglou .... (1896-1965)
- Andrew Georgiadis (the "Cretan") .... (1892-1981)
- Spyros Vassiliou .... (1902-1985)
- Nicolas Hadzikyriakos-Guikas .... (1906-   )
- John Spyropoulos .... (1912-   )
- Nike Karagatsi .... (1914-1986)

Some of the most famous sculptors of modern Greece at the Art National Gallery

- John Cossos .... (1822-1875)
  (Statue of Rigas Ferraios, forerunner of the Independence, in front of Athens University).
- George Phytalis .... (middle XIX c.)
  (Statue of the Patriarch of Constantinople Gregory V, in front of Athens University.
- Leonidas Drossis .... (1834-1882)
  (Statue of Plato in front of the Academy in Athens, and statues of Athena and Apollo on the columns of the Academy, and the reliefs of the pediments of this building.
- George Vroutos .... (1843-1909)
- Dem. Philippotis .... (1839-1919)
  ("The wood-cutter", opposite the Athens marble Stadium).
- John Halepas .... (1851-1938)
  ("The sleeping girl"), funeral statue in the Ist cemetery, in Athens.

— Lazarus Sohos .... (1862-1911)
(Monumental statue of Theodore Kolokotronis, in front of the Old Parliament, Stadiou st., and in the central park of Nauplia - gold medallion, Paris 1900).
— Anthony Sohos .... (1888-1975)
— Mich. Tombros .... (1889-1974)
— Const. Dimitriadis .... (1881-1943)
(The Discobolus, in front of the marble Stadium in Athens, and the monumental statue of the bishop-martyr Chrysostom of Smyrna, tortured by the Turks in 1922, behind the Cathedral of Athens).
— Phocion Roque .... (1891-1945)
(Warrior during the liberation of Epirus. He created the "Tomb of the Unknown Soldier", in front of the façade of the Parliament in Athens, and the statue of Chateaubriand, (King Constantine Ave., close to the War Museum).
— Athan. Apartis .... (1889-1972)
— George Castriotis .... (1899-1969)
(80 of his works are in the Town - Hall of Piraeus as donation)
— Basil Phaliréas .... (1905-1979)
(Leonidas at Thermopylae, Leonidas in Sparta, and the National poet Costis Palamas, statue in marble behind the University, in Athens).
— Ann Bekiari .... (1895-1969)

Some composers of classical music of modern Greece

— Paul Karrère .... (1829-1899)
— Dion. Lavragas .... (1864-1941)
(Creator of the Modern-Greek Opera
— Sp. Samaras .... (1861-1917)
— George Labelet .... (1875-1945)
— Manolis Kalomiris .... (1883-1962)
(Creator of the Classical Modern-Greek music)
— Marius Varvoglis .... (1885-1902)
— Aimilios Riadis .... (1886-1936)
— P. Petridis .... (1892-   )
— Nicolas Scalotas .... (1904-1949)

- Ant. Evanguelatos .... (1903-)
- Menelaos Pallandios (Member of the Academy) ... (1914-)
- John Christou .... (1926-1970)
- Th. Andoniou .... (1935-)
- Dem. Mitropoulos .... (1896- 1960)
  (Composer and famous orchestra Director)
- John Xenakis .... (1921-)
  (Music based on mathematics)
- Solon Michailidis (from Cyprus) .... (1905-1979)

Some writers and poets of modern Greece translated in English

- "Loukis Laras", by Dem. Vikelas (Novel of the period of the Greek Independence), London, Doric Publications, 1972.
- "Folk Songs of Greece "(with music notes), by Suzan and Ted Alevizos, Oak Publications, 78, Newman st. London W.I.P. 3LA, 1968.
- "The Greek Folk Songs", by Niki Watts, Bristol Cl. Press U.K., 1988.
- "Modern Greek Poetry", by Kimon Friar, Pub. Efstathiadis and Sons S.A. Athens, (14, Valtetsiou st. Tel. 3615011).
- "Voices of Modern Greeks". Trans. by Edm. Keely and Philip Sherrard, Prinston University Press, 1981.
- "Modern Greek music and Poetry" (Anthology) by K. Mitsakis, Publ. Grigoris, Athens 1979.
- "The King's flute", by Kostes Palamas, transl. by T.P. Stefanides, Publ. "Kostes Palamas Institute", Athens, 1982.
- "Kostes Palamas, His life & Work", by Robin A. Tletcher, Publ. "Kostes Palamas Institute", Athens 1984.
- "Exile and Return", by Yannis Ritsos, (selected poems 1967-1974), transl. by Edm. Keeley, Publ. The Ecco Press, 1985.
- "Selected Poems, by Yannis Ritsos, transl. by Nikis Stanges, Athens 1983. Distrib. Efstathiadis Group, 14, Valtetsiou st. Athens, Tel. 3615.011).
- "Collected Poems" by George Seferis, transl. by Edm. Keeley and Philip Sherrard, Publ. Avril Press Poetry, London, 1982.

- "On the Greek style and Hellenism", by George Seferis sellected essays on poetry), publ. Denise Harvey and Co. Athens 1966.
- "Collected Poems", by K. Cavafy, transl. by Edm. Keeley and Philip Sherrard, Publ. the Hogarth Press, London, 1974.
- "Greek Women Poets", transl. Award Fourtani.
- "The Axion esti", by Odysseus Elytis, transl. and annotated, by Edm. Keeley and George Savidis, Publ. Avril Press, London, 1980.
- "Maria Nephele". A poem in two voices, by Odysseus Elytis, transl. by Athan. Anagnostopoulos, Boston U.S.A., Houghton Mifflin, 1981.
- "Selected Poems" by Odysseus Elytis, transl. by Edm. Keeley, Philip Sherrard, Penguin Books, 1981.
- "The Penguin Book of Greek verse" Introduced and edited by Const. Trypanis. Great Britain, 1971.
- "Greek poetry" by Raizis Byron (translations, views etc.), Athens, 1981.
- "Cypriote Prose-writers from antiquity to 1950", by Nicos S. Spanos, Nicosia-Cyprus, 1983.
- "The wound of Greece" (Studies in Neo-Hellenism), by Philip Sherrard, Publ. Rex Collings, London 1978.
- "God's Pauper" (St. Francis of Assisi), by Nicos Kazandzakis, 1988.
- "Freedom and death", by Nicos Kazandzakis, Faber and Faber, London 1987.
- Zorba the Greek by Nicos Kazandzakis, Faber and Faber, London 1988.
- "By fire and axe", by Evangelos Averoff-Tossizza, transl. by Sarah Arnold - Rigos. Publ. Karatzas Bros, New York, 1978.
- "Aeolia", by Venezis Ilias, transl. by E.D. Scott-Kilvert, Campion Ed. London, 1949.
- "A history of modern Greek literature", by C. Dimaras, transl. by Mary Gianos. Albany, University of New York Press, 1972.
- "The Herb of Love", by G. Drossinis, transl. by E.M. Edmonds, London 1982.
- "Argo", a novel by G. Theotokas, transl. by E. Margaret Brooke, Methuen, London, 1951.
- "Memoirs from the Greek War of Independence" by Theod.

171

Kolokotronis (1821-1833). Transl. by E.M. Edmonds, Chicago, Argonaut, 1969.

— "Memoirs of General Makriyannis" (1797-1864). Transl. by H.A. Liddersdale. London, 1966.

— "The Schoolmistress with the golden eyes", by Stratis Myrivilis, transl. by Philip Sherrard. Hutchinson, London 1964, Efstadiadis, Athens 1981.

— "The childrens inferno", Lilika Nacos, (Stories of the great famine in Greece), transl. Allan Ross MacDougall, Hollywood, Gateway Books, 1946.

— "The contemporary man", by I. M. Panayotopoulos, transl. by Maria P. Hogan Vantage Press, New York, 1970.

— "The murderess" by Alex. Papadiamantis, transl. by G. Xanthopoulides. Publ. Athens, Doric Publications, 1977.

— "The sun of death", by Pandel. Prevelakis, transl. by Philip Sherrard, London, Murray, 1965.

— "Hours on Sinai", by Tsatsos Ioanna, transl. by Jean Demos, Hellenic College Press, Brookline, Mass. 1984.

SELECTED BIBLIOGRAPHY

Ancient Greece

— "Greece and its Myths", by Michael Senior, Pub. Victor Collancz Ltd. 1978.

— "A Traveller's guide - Structure and History in Greek Mythology and ritual, by Walter Burkert, Pub. University of California Press, Paper-back 1982.

— "Mythology", by Edith Hamilton, A Mentor Book, publ. by Little, Brown and Co. Boston, Mass. 1969.

— "A History of Greece - to the death of Alexander the Great", by G.B. Bury. Publ. by Random House Inc. in the U.S.A., 1913.

— The Pelican History of Greece" by R. Burn, Penguin Books, 1966.

— "The Archeology of Greece, by William R. Biers, Publ. Cornell University Press, Ithaca & London 1987.

— "The Greek Stones speak", by Paul MacKendrick, Publ. W.W. Norton & Co. 1981.

— "Greek Architecture", by Roland Martin, Publ. Faber & Faber, 1988.
— "The Greek Polis", by Arthur W.H. Adkin & Peter White, (Readings in Western civilisation), University of Chicago Press, 1986.
— "Canon of Greek Authors & Works" by Luci Berkowitz & Karl A. Squitier, Publ. Oxford University Press, 1986.
— "The Oxford Companion to Classical Literature", by Sir Paul Harvey, Oxford, at the Clarendon Press, 1959.
— "The Pelican History of Greek Literature" by Peter Levi, Penguin Books, 1985.
— "The Greek way", by Edith Hamilton, Discus books, Avon, New York, 1973.
— "The Greek experience", by C.M. Bowra, A Mentor Book, New York, 1963.
— "Landmarks in Greeks literature" Penguin Books, 1968.
— "The Greeks", by H.D.F. Kitto, Penguin Books, 1964.
— "The Greeks overseas", by John Boardman, Penguin Books, 1964.
— "Prehistoric Crete", by R.W. Hutchinson, Penguin Books, 1965.
— "The Bull of Minos", by Leonard Cottrell, Pan Books Ltd, London, 1960.
— "Pausanias-Guide to Greece", vol. I.II., Penguin Books 1971.
— Arrian, "The campaigns of Alexander", Penguin Books 1971.
— Apollonius of Rhodes, "The voyage of Argo". Penguin Books, 1971.
— "Greek Science", by Benjamin Farrington, Penguin Books, 1963.
— "The World of Odysseus"; by M.I. Finley, Penguin Books 1956.
— "The Delphic Oracle", with a catalogue of responses. by Joseph Fontenrose. Publ. University of California Press.
— "A History of Macedonia" by N.G.L. Hammond. Oxford, Clarendon Press, 1972.
— "A History of Epirus", by N.G.L. Hammond.
— "Macedonia, 4.000 years of Greek History and Civilisation", general Editor M.B. Sakellariou, Member of the Academy of Athens, Publ. Ekdotiki, Athens 1983.

Byzantine Greece

— "History of the Byzantine State" by, George Ostogorsky, Publ. Basil Blackwell, reprinted 1986.
— "The fall of Constantinople in 1453", by Steven Runciman, Cambridge University Press, 1982.
— "The Great Church in Captivity", by Steven Runciman, Cambridge University Press, 1988.
— "The History of the Church" by Eusebius (IV c. A.D.) transl. by G.A. Williamson, publ. Dorset Press, 1983. Penguin books, 1983.
— "Early Christian writings", (the Apostolic Fathers, II c. A.D.), Penguin Books, 1981.
— "Dictionary of Saints", by Donald Attwater, Penguin Books, 1983.
— "A Treasury of Early Christianity", by Anne Fremantle, Mentor Book, U.S.A. 1953.
— "The Early Church", by Henry Chadwick, Penguin Books, 1978.
— "The Origins of Christian Art", by Michael Gough, Thames & Hudson, London 1973.
— "The Mosaics on Nea Moni on Chios Vol. I, II., Commerc. Bank of Greece, 1985.
— Different books on Byzantine Art (Mosaics, frescoes, icons) by Talbot Rice.
— "Aghia Sophia". Rowland J. Mainstone, Publ. Thames & Hudson, 1988.
— Library of the Fathers", Busey-Keeble, Oxford, 1838-1888.
— "Fathers of the Church", Sechopp-Walsh & Deferrari, New York 1947.
— "Greek Authors ancient and Medieval" Publ. Loeb. U.S.A.
— "The Orthodox Church" by Tim. Ware, Penguin Books, 1967.
— "The Orthodox Church" by John Meyendorff, publ. Darton, Longman & Todd, London, 1960.
— "Church Papacy and Schism", by Philip Sherrard. Publ. SPCK, London 1978.
— "Differences between the Orthodox Church & Roman Catholicism, by Irene Economides (reprint 1988), 34,

Astydamandos st. Athens 116.34, Greece, Tel. 7228-486, 7231-992.
- "Our Orthodox Christian Faith", by Athanasios S. Frangopoulos, publ. Brotherhood of Theologians "O SOTIR" (the Saviour"), 42, Isavron st. Athens 114.72-Greece.
- "Church World Mission", by Alexander Schmemann, Publ. S. Vladimir, Seminary Press, Crestwood, NY. 10707. 1979.
- "The Byzantine Legacy in Eastern Europe", by Lowell Chucas, Publ. Eastern European Monographs, U.S.A. 1988.

- Artistic Guide-books, publ. "Ekdotiki", Omirou st. Athens.

Modern Greece

- "Modern Greece - A Short History" by C.M. Woodhouse, Publ. Faber & Faber London - Boston, 1984.
- "Modern Greece", by John Cambell & Philip Sherrard, Publ. Ernest Benn Ltd. London, 1968.
- "British Policy towards Greece during the II World War" (1941-44), by Procopis Papastratis. Publ. Cambridge University Press, 1984.
- "Greece in the 1980s", by Richard Clogg, Publ. the Mc Millan Press Ltd. London, 1983.
- "American Intervention in Greece" (1943-1949), by Lawrence S. Wittner, Columbia University Press N.Y. 1982.
- History of the Greek Revolution and the reign of King Otho", by George Finlay, Publ. Zeno, 1971.
- "Count John Capodistria" (first governor of Independent Greece), by G.M. Woodhouse. Oxford University Press, London, 1973.
- "Revolt in Athens" (1944-45), by John O., Iatrides, Princeton University Press, 1972.
- "The Greek Economy in the XX c.", by A.T. Freris, Publ. Croom Helm, London & Sydney, 1986.
- "The Festivals of Greek Easter", by Carol Papoutsis, (Distr. 16, Karatza st. Philopapou - Athens, Tel. 923.7650), 1972.
- "Greek Dances", by Ted Petrides, Lycabettus Press, P.O. Box 3391, Athens, 1980.

- "The world of Greek dance", by Alkis Raftis, Finedawn Publishers, London, 1987.
- "Music in the Aegean", Ministry of culture, Athens, 1987.
- "The Greek Shadow-Theatre" (Karaghiozis), Publ. Gnosis, 29 Zoodochou Pighis, Athens 106.11, 1986.
- "Greek Folk Costumes", by Angeliki Hadzimichali, Publ. MELISSA, 10, Navarinou st. 10680 Athens, vol. I. 1979, vol. II 1983.
- "Greek Threadwork (lace), 1989. Publ. MELISSA, 10 Navarinou st. 10680 Athens.
- "Greek Traditional jewelry, 1980. Publ. MELISSA, 10, Navarinou st. 10680 Athens.
- "Greek Sailing ships (Museum of Galaxidi), 1988. Publ. MELISSA, 10, Navarinou st. 10680 Athens.
- "Greek painting (XIX c.), 1974. Publ. MELISSA, 10, Navarinou st. 10680 Athens.
- "Greek Traditional Architecture, I, II, 1983. Publ. MELISSA 10, Navarinou st. 10680 Athens.
- "Historical Album of the Greek Revolution", 1974. Publ. MELISSA 10, Navarinou st. 10680 Athens.
- "Modern Greek Thought", by Const. Cavarnos, Istitute for Byzantine and Modern Greek studies. 115, Gilbert Road, Belmont, Mass. 02178.
- "Crucified Northern Epirus" by bishop. Sevastianos, distr. "SOTIR" 100 Solonos st. Athens.

On Cyprus

- "Cyprus, from the Stone Age to the Romans". by Vassos Karageorghis, Publ. Thames & Hudson, 1982.
- "History of Cyprus", by Costas. D. Kypris. Publ. Nicolls, Nicosia, 1983.
- "Cyprus, the country and its people", by Celia Henderson, Queen Anne Press, 1968.
- "Cyprus 1958-1967", by Thomas Ehrilich, Oxford University Press, 1974.
- "Background notes on Cyprus" issued by "Jus Cypris", Nicosia 1976.

CONTENTS

177

By the same author

— First translation of the "Little Prince" by Ant. de St. Exu-péry, in Modern Greek (Forword: by Roger Milliex, Vice-Director of the French Institute in Athens, where the author was working then as teacher of French), Ed. "Difros", Athens 1957.

— "Legends of Greece Ancient and Modern", Athens, 1965 (in French), (1967 in English), published by the author for the visitors of Greece. (Out of print).

— Differences between the Orthodox Church and Roman Catholicism" Athens, 1980 in French, (4th French edition revised 1987) - (4th English ed. 1988). Dist. Irene Economides, 34, Astydamandos st. Athens 116. 34.

— "The Liturgy of St. John Chrysostom (IV c. A.D.), tran-slated in Modern literary Greek for the children", 1983 (8th Ed. 1988) Pub. "Tinos" 6, Valsamonos st. Athens 114.71, Tel. 6425.998. (Authorized by the Ecumenical Patriarchate of Constantinople).

— "Let there be light": Three hundred poems in the Greek traditional style written in 25 years (1960-1985) during the professional travels of the author throughout Greece and the coasts of Asia Minor. Poetic voyage inspired by the history, and civilisation of Greece, Athens 1985. Dist. Irene Economidès, 34, Astydamandos st. Athens 116. 34. This book obtained a distinction in 1986 by "The Christian Literary Company", in Athens (not yet translated).

— "The two faces of Greece" (in French), Athens 1988, published by the author.

Γραφικες Τεχνες
γιωργος παπανικολαου & Σια Ο.Ε.
ιπποκρατους 71-106 80 αθηνα
τηλ 3624728-3609342